THE W
Professional Whis

MW01532040

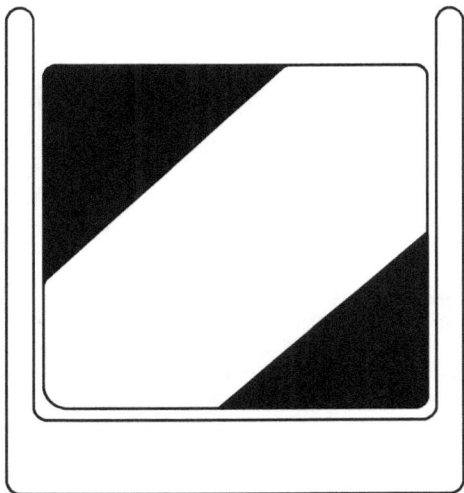

First Edition, 2020
ISBN 978-1-63649-021-2

For orders or sales enquiries please visit www.artisandoodlebooks.com

or email hello@artisandoodlebooks.com

This Doodle Book is dedicated to all dogs. That's right. Just any dog, anywhere.
They truly are the best friends to us. Give your dog a hug.

THE WHISKEY TASTING DOODLE BOOK™

A professional whisky tasting journal for scribblers, doodlers and drawers

by Joshua James

First of all, thank you for supporting the Whiskey Tasting Doodle Book!

As a young man growing up in the north of England, I always thought of our friends in the far north to be occupants of a near-magical land. Anyone who has visited Scotland will probably attest to this, and when I first made my way to the highlands to enjoy my first dram of whisky this was wholeheartedly confirmed. Rolling hills, stunning lakes and gorgeous lore all combined to make my first distillery visit a dream come true. The craftsmanship that went into the whisky itself transported me to a new level of artisanal appreciation and obsession.

Now, after traveling and tasting my way through Scotland, Ireland, Canada, Europe and North America, I would say it is safe to say I am completely in awe of the Aqua Vitae, or Water of Life. On those travels I found myself trying to depict whisky flavors by drawing how it made me feel, rather than just writing down the words. I would scribble, doodle and draw, creating a new way to take my tasting notes, and I loved the results. That was how I got the idea for this doodle book. It is a way for creatives like us to express ourselves in new ways while appreciating the nuances of the whiskeys before us. So to you, I raise a glass of whiskey, or whisky. I hope you enjoy your tasting journey, and here's to many more doodles and incredible drams!

-Joshua James

HOW TO USE THIS DOODLE BOOK

It's super easy to use. Write on the lines, color anything that has space to do so, and doodle whenever you see big boxes! It's up to you how you use it, but we've drawn a quick guide below to get you started. The journal pages are divided into 4 sections - Appearance, Aroma, Taste and Other Thoughts - a common structure used by whisky tasters and distillers the world over. Enjoy!

Color these in depending on which glass you are using (and if you like, how much you have in the glass.)———→

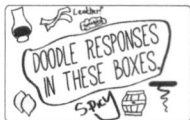

DOODLE RESPONSES IN THESE BOXES.

NOTES *WRITE ALL OF YOUR NOTES, IDEAS AND TIPS ON THESE LINES. WHATEVER WORKS FOR YOU.*

Mark these with a dash to indicate the level. It varies depending on the scale.

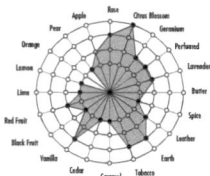

Starting from the center rate each item from 0 - 5 going outwards. Join the dots and color it in to get an aroma pattern.

Color up to the correct description.

Leave the answer blank. Color in the rest. Easy!

Color in.   GOLDEN   AMBER   TAWNY

And these.

These too.   👍

Yep.

WHISKEY TASTING TERMINOLOGY

Although designed to be a fun experience we still wanted to create a great tool for learning; so with that in mind we penned this quick glossary to make sure you're always using the correct whiskey terminology and you'll fully understand all of the terms we use throughout the book.

ABV - Alcohol by by Volume. Refers to what percentage of the given liquid - whiskey in this case - is alcohol.

Age - Sometimes a bottle will display in years how long the whiskey has been aged.

Angels Share - Roughly 2% of each barrel of whiskey is lost to porous wood and evaporation. This was said to go to the heavens and be 'The Angels Share'.

Barrel - Large cylindrical wooden casks held together with metal rings used for aging whiskey. Flavor and aroma are both imparted from the barrel itself. Barrel makers are known as coopers.

Bourbon - A type of whiskey invented in the US which uses charred barrels and at least 51% Corn, with the rest being malt and rye.

Blend - A whiskey made from blending multiple whiskeys, and/or adding grain spirits or flavorings to a whiskey.

Char/Charred - Sometimes the inside of the whiskey barrel is charred to impart smokey notes to the whiskey during the aging process.

Corn - A cereal grain used in the production of whiskey (and many other things such as beer, snack goods, sweeteners, etc). Especially prevalent to Bourbon, as it makes up 51% or more of the mash.

Congener - Congeners are chemical byproducts produced during fermentation and distillation other than the desired alcohol. These can be tannins, methanol, acetone and many others, and are partly responsible for individual flavors and aromas in different whiskeys.

Bottled-In-Bond - The spirit must be aged for at least four years, then bottled at precisely 100 proof (50% ABV). It must have been made by one distiller at a single distillery in a single season, then aged in a bonded warehouse.

Distillation - In whiskey, distillation is the process of extracting the alcohol created during fermentation. This concentrated spirit will go on to be matured into the final product.

Distillers Beer - The alcoholic beer that is made through fermentation in the early stage of whiskey making. This is then distilled to produce spirit, and the spirit then aged in barrels.

WHISKEY TASTING TERMINOLOGY

Dram -   Dram - Technically, a dram is a measurement 1/8 of a fluid ounce of whisky, but it has now evolved to mean any small amount of whisky or other spirit.

Ethanol -   Ethanol - Short for ethyl alcohol. It is the clear, flammable liquid created during fermentation that we drink in our whiskey and spirits.

Fermentation -   Fermentation - The process of yeast breaking down sugars and converting them into CO_2 and ethanol. This is a necessary step for all whiskey (and beer).

Finger -   Finger - An imperfect measurement of whiskey, where you use your finger as a guide for the pour.

Irish Whiskey -   Developed and produced in Ireland. Must be aged for at least 3 years in wooden casks and made from malted cereal grains. The word 'whiskey' comes from the Irish ('Gaelic') uisce beatha, meaning water of life.

Japanese Whisky -   Developed and produced in Japan. Production started in 1870, but commercial production took off in 1924. The majority of Japanese whisky is similar to scotch in its production, although trends are changing and Japan continues to innovate and impress the world market.

Malt -   A cereal grain that has been dried and partly germinated in a process known as malting, ready for fermentation. The malt contains the fermentable sugars which the yeast will convert into alcohol.

Nose -   Using your sense of smell to evaluate whiskey. The more you practice sniffing whisky the better at describing the aromas you will become.

Oak -   What the large majority of whiskey barrels are made of. It imparts color and flavor from the wood. Even more so if charred, and more again if it has previously been used by another spirit or liquor.

Oxidation -   When whiskey is exposed to ambient oxygen. This happens as soon as the bottle is opened, and oxidation helps improve aroma and flavor, which is why we let whiskey breathe. However, too much oxidation leads to off-flavors.

Peat/Peated -   A soil-like moss deposit that is cultivated and added to whiskey to give it a smokey flavor. Found in abundance in Scotland, it is what gives scotch its distinctive taste.

Proof -   An alternative measure of alcohol to ABV. Proof is double the alcohol content, so 100 proof whiskey would be 50% ABV (Alcohol By Volume).

WHISKEY TASTING TERMINOLOGY

Single Malt - A whiskey made at only one distillery. In the UK, it must also be made using pot stills and aged for at least three years in oak casks not exceeding 700 liters (180 US gallons).

Small Batch - A loose term for creating a small amount of whiskey using a select amount of the same type of barrel. There is currently no legal definition.

Still - The apparatus used to distill sprit from the distillers beer.

Straight - Refers to a spirit distilled from cereal grain mash to a concentrate that does not exceed 80% ABV and is then aged in charred oak barrels for at least two years.

Unicorn - A term used by whiskey fans to refer to a rare or difficult to find whiskey. Sometimes considered once in a lifetime experiences!

Wheat - A cereal grain used to make whiskey. Wheat can also be used as a flavor-adding ingredient in whiskey such as 'wheated bourbon'.

Whisky/ Whiskey - What this doodle book celebrates! An alcoholic beverage made from distilling fermented grain mash. Cheers!

ADD YOUR OWN

MORE ABOUT WHISKEY
Barrel size and Oak Type

125 Litres

Quarter Cask

200 Litres

ASB – American
Standard Barrel

250 Litres

Hogshead

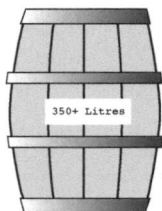

350+ Litres

Port Pipe

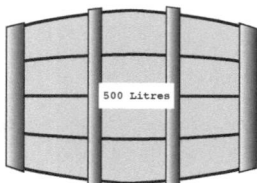

500 Litres

Butt

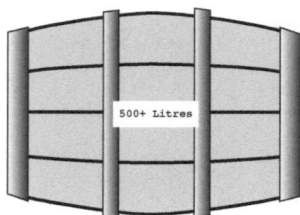

500+ Litres

Puncheon

HOW TO READ THE LABEL

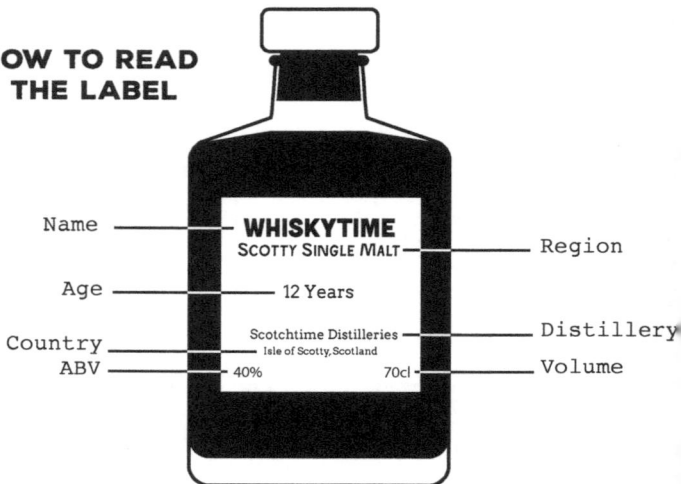

Name — **WHISKYTIME**
SCOTTY SINGLE MALT — Region

Age — 12 Years

Scotchtime Distilleries — Distillery
Country — Isle of Scotty, Scotland
ABV — 40%   70cl — Volume

A QUICK GUIDE TO POPULAR WHISKEY TYPES

Know your Grains, Barrels and Blends

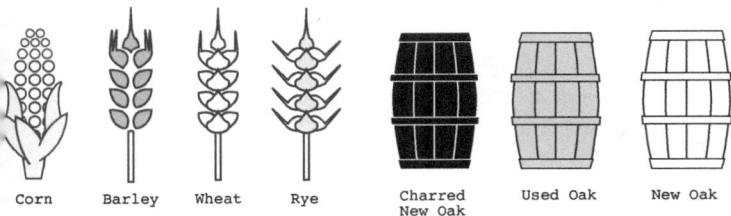

Corn	Barley	Wheat	Rye	Charred New Oak	Used Oak	New Oak

Bourbon	American Rye	Straight Rye	Single Malt(UK)
+ 8%+ 0+ Years	+ 51%+ 2+ Years	+ 51%+ 2+ Years Unblended	+ 100% 3+ Years

Scotch Whisky	Single Grain	Irish Whiskey
+ and/ or + 3+ Years	or or or + 100% 0+ Years	+ + 30% Malted 30% Unmalted 0+ Years

Blended Scotch	Blended Malt	Corn	Straight Wheat
Single Grain + Single Malt	Single Malt + Single Malt	+ 80%+ 0+ Years	+ 51%+ 2+ Years

DOODLES & NOTES

THE WHISKEY TASTING DOODLE BOOK™

WHISKEY LOG

Use these pages to log your whiskeys and create an easy way to search through the pages. At the bottom right corner of every journal page there is a box. Number, letter or doodle something in it, then add a corresponding sign on this page. Voila! Instant flickbook searching.

WHISKEY NAME	DATE	LOG SYMBOL
Jim Beam Black Extra Aged	12/30/20	JB1

WHISKEY LOG (CONTINUED)

WHISKEY NAME	DATE	LOG SYMBOL

Distillery **Jim Bean** Region _____

Whiskey Name **Black Extra Aged** Country **USA**

Type **Kentucky Straight Bourbon** ABV **43%**

Age **O** Unicorn? 👍 Rating 🥃🥃🥃🥃🥃

APPEARANCE - First, fill your glass! (Or draw your own)

Swirling Glass | Vinum Single Malt | Large Glencairn | NEAT Glass | Wine | Glencairn | Straight Tumbler | Bourbon Tumbler | Draw Your Own!

Now, hold it up against a white background. Describe what you see.

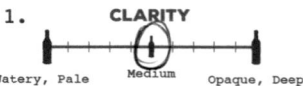

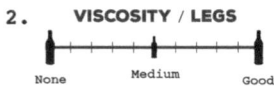

1. CLARITY

Watery, Pale — Medium — Opaque, Deep

2. VISCOSITY / LEGS

None — Medium — Good

3. COLOR & HUE

Gin Clear	Pale Straw	Light Gold
Yellow Gold	Golden	Pale Amber
Rich Amber	Burnt Amber	Tawny
Mahogany	Old Oak	Treacle

Lighter / ld/Amber / Darker

4. DOODLES & NOTES

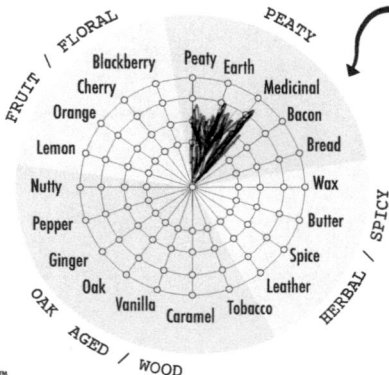

AROMA - Let's get your nose involved. Use the Aroma Wheel.

DOODLES & NOTES

FRUIT / FLORAL — PEATY — HERBAL / SPICY — OAK / AGED / WOOD

Blackberry, Cherry, Orange, Lemon, Nutty, Pepper, Ginger, Oak, Vanilla, Caramel, Tobacco, Leather, Spice, Butter, Wax, Bread, Bacon, Medicinal, Earth, Peaty

TASTE - OK, now take a sip. Roll it around. Describe it.

1. FIRST TASTE

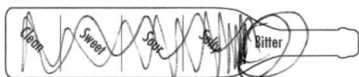
Clean | Sweet | Spice | Sour | Bitter

2. FLAVOR

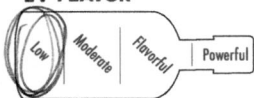
Low | Moderate | Flavorful | Powerful

3. PEATY

None | Low | Medium | High | Extreme

4. BODY

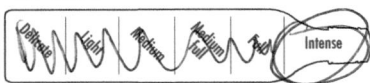
Delicate | Light | Medium | Medium Full | Full | Intense

5. SWEETNESS

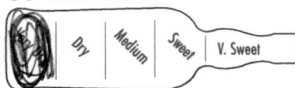
Dry | Medium | Sweet | V. Sweet

DOODLES & NOTES

Burn

6. FLAVOR GRAPH

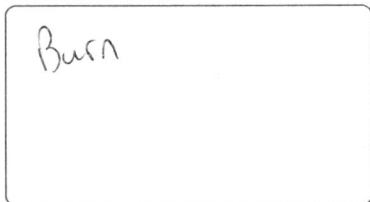
Smokey
Light | Rich
Delicate

MARK WITH A

7. FINISH

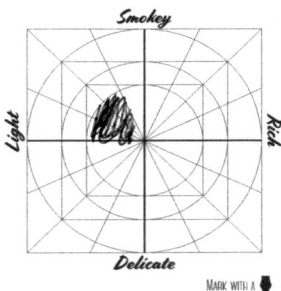
V. Long | Short | Long | Medium

Describe it

Sits there

8. BALANCE

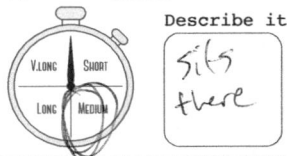
Not Balanced | Balanced | Harmonious | Complex

9. DEPTH

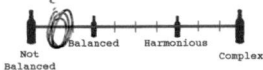
None | Medium | Great

10. OFF-FLAVORS?

OTHER THOUGHTS - What did you think of this one?

BOTTLE & LABEL

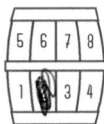
5 6 7 8
1 2 3 4

VALUE

5 6 7 8
1 2 3 4

PRICE

DRINK AGAIN?

DESCRIBE IN 3 WORDS

Burn
Earthy
Watery Eyes

LOG: JB 1

Distillery _____ Region _____

Whiskey Name _____ Country _____

Type _____ ABV _____

Age _____ Unicorn? 👍 Rating 🥃🥃🥃🥃🥃

APPEARANCE - First, fill your glass! (Or draw your own)

Swirling Glass | Vinum Single Malt | Large Glencairn | NEAT Glass | Wine | Glencairn | Straight Tumbler | Bourbon Tumbler | Draw Your Own!

Now, hold it up against a white background. Describe what you see.

1. CLARITY

Watery, Pale — Medium — Opaque, Deep

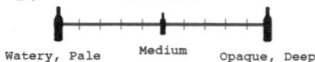

2. VISCOSITY / LEGS

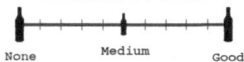

None — Medium — Good

3. COLOR & HUE

Lighter / d/Amber / Darker

Gin Clear	Pale Straw	Light Gold
Yellow Gold	Golden	Pale Amber
Rich Amber	Burnt Amber	Tawny
Mahogany	Old Oak	Treacle

4. DOODLES & NOTES

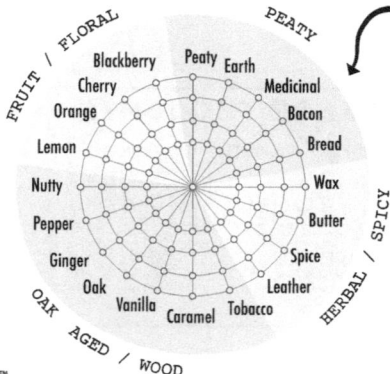

AROMA - Let's get your nose involved. Use the Aroma Wheel.

DOODLES & NOTES

FRUIT / FLORAL: Blackberry, Cherry, Orange, Lemon

PEATY: Peaty Earth, Medicinal, Bacon, Bread

SPICY: Wax, Butter, Spice, Leather

HERBAL / SPICY

Nutty, Pepper, Ginger, Oak, Vanilla, Caramel, Tobacco

OAK / AGED / WOOD

THE WHISKEY TASTING DOODLE BOOK™

TASTE - OK, now take a sip. Roll it around. Describe it.

1. FIRST TASTE

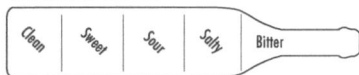

Clean | Sweet | Sour | Salty | Bitter

2. FLAVOR

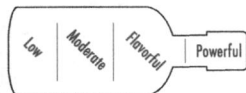

Low | Moderate | Flavorful | Powerful

3. PEATY

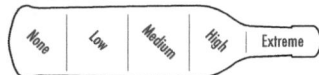

None | Low | Medium | High | Extreme

4. BODY

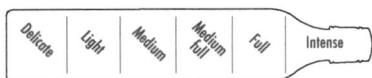

Delicate | Light | Medium | Medium Full | Full | Intense

5. SWEETNESS

Very Dry | Dry | Medium | Sweet | V. Sweet

DOODLES & NOTES

6. FLAVOR GRAPH

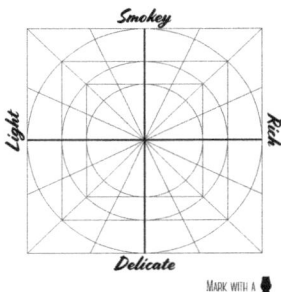

Smokey
Light
Rich
Delicate

MARK WITH A 🖤

7. FINISH

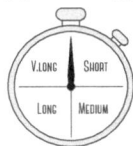

V. LONG | SHORT
LONG | MEDIUM

Describe it

8. BALANCE

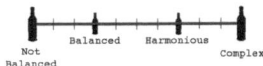

Not Balanced | Balanced | Harmonious | Complex

9. DEPTH

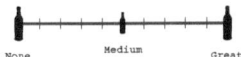

None | Medium | Great

10. OFF-FLAVORS?

OTHER THOUGHTS - What did you think of this one?

BOTTLE & LABEL

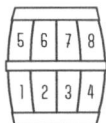

5 | 6 | 7 | 8
1 | 2 | 3 | 4

VALUE

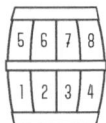

5 | 6 | 7 | 8
1 | 2 | 3 | 4

PRICE

DRINK AGAIN?

DESCRIBE IN 3 WORDS

_____

_____

_____

LOG:

Distillery _____ Region _____

Whiskey Name _____ Country _____

Type _____ ABV _____

Age _____ Unicorn? 👍 Rating 🥃🥃🥃🥃🥃

APPEARANCE - First, fill your glass! (Or draw your own)

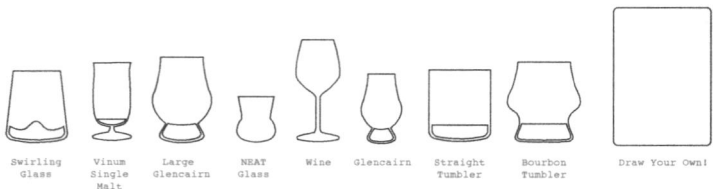

Swirling Glass | Vinum Single Malt | Large Glencairn | NEAT Glass | Wine | Glencairn | Straight Tumbler | Bourbon Tumbler | Draw Your Own!

Now, hold it up against a white background. Describe what you see

1. CLARITY

Watery, Pale — Medium — Opaque, Deep

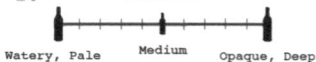

2. VISCOSITY / LEGS

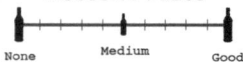

None — Medium — Good

3. COLOR & HUE

Lighter Gold/Amber Darker

Gin Clear	Pale Straw	Light Gold
Yellow Gold	Golden	Pale Amber
Rich Amber	Burnt Amber	Tawny
Mahogany	Old Oak	Treacle

4. DOODLES & NOTES

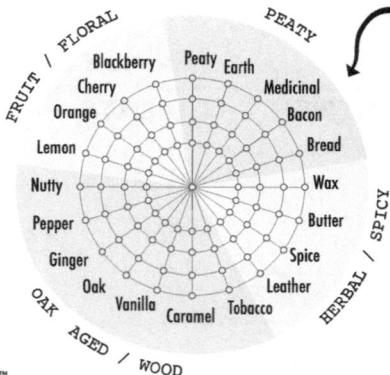

AROMA - Let's get your nose involved. Use the Aroma Wheel.

DOODLES & NOTES

FRUIT / FLORAL — PEATY — SPICY — HERBAL / SPICY — OAK AGED / WOOD

Blackberry, Cherry, Orange, Lemon, Nutty, Pepper, Ginger, Oak, Vanilla, Caramel, Tobacco, Leather, Spice, Butter, Wax, Bread, Bacon, Medicinal, Earth, Peaty

THE WHISKEY TASTING DOODLE BOOK™

TASTE - OK, now take a sip. Roll it around. Describe it.

1. FIRST TASTE

Clean | Sweet | Sour | Salty | Bitter

2. FLAVOR

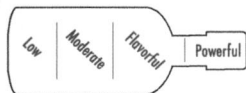

Low | Moderate | Flavorful | Powerful

3. PEATY

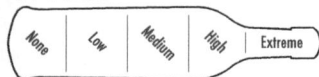

None | Low | Medium | High | Extreme

4. BODY

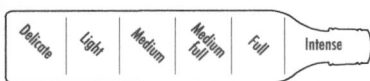

Delicate | Light | Medium | Medium full | Full | Intense

5. SWEETNESS

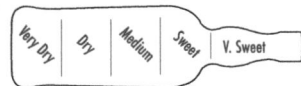

Very Dry | Dry | Medium | Sweet | V. Sweet

DOODLES & NOTES

6. FLAVOR GRAPH

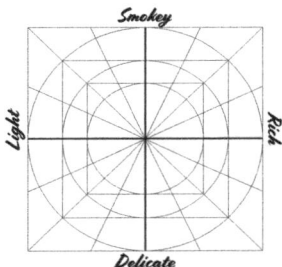

Smokey

Light

Rich

Delicate

MARK WITH A 🖤

7. FINISH

V. LONG | SHORT
LONG | MEDIUM

Describe it

8. BALANCE

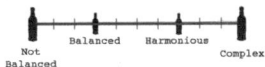

Not Balanced | Balanced | Harmonious | Complex

9. DEPTH

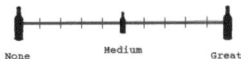

None | Medium | Great

10. OFF-FLAVORS?

OTHER THOUGHTS - What did you think of this one?

BOTTLE & LABEL

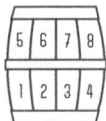

5 | 6 | 7 | 8
1 | 2 | 3 | 4

VALUE

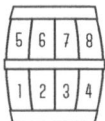

5 | 6 | 7 | 8
1 | 2 | 3 | 4

PRICE

DRINK AGAIN?

DESCRIBE IN 3 WORDS

_____
_____
_____

THE WHISKEY TASTING DOODLE BOOK™

LOG:

Distillery _____	Region _____
Whiskey Name _____	Country _____
Type _____	ABV _____
Age _____ Unicorn? 👍	Rating ⟨⟩⟨⟩⟨⟩⟨⟩⟨⟩

APPEARANCE - First, fill your glass! (Or draw your own)

Swirling Glass | Vinum Single Malt | Large Glencairn | NEAT Glass | Wine | Glencairn | Straight Tumbler | Bourbon Tumbler | Draw Your Own!

Now, hold it up against a white background. Describe what you see

1.   CLARITY

Watery, Pale — Medium — Opaque, Deep

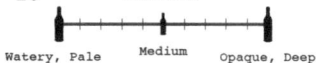

2.   VISCOSITY / LEGS

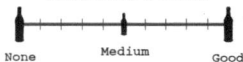

None — Medium — Good

3.   COLOR & HUE

Lighter
Gold/Amber
Darker

Gin Clear	Pale Straw	Light Gold
Yellow Gold	Golden	Pale Amber
Rich Amber	Burnt Amber	Tawny
Mahogany	Old Oak	Treacle

4.   DOODLES & NOTES

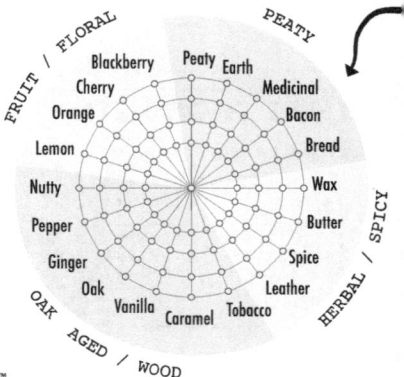

AROMA - Let's get your nose involved. Use the Aroma Wheel.

DOODLES & NOTES

FRUIT / FLORAL — PEATY
HERBAL / SPICY
OAK AGED / WOOD

Blackberry Peaty Earth
Cherry Medicinal
Orange Bacon
Lemon Bread
Nutty Wax
Pepper Butter
Ginger Spice
Oak Leather
Vanilla Caramel Tobacco

THE WHISKEY TASTING DOODLE BOOK™

TASTE - OK, now take a sip. Roll it around. Describe it.

1. FIRST TASTE

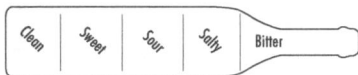

Clean | Sweet | Sour | Salty | Bitter

2. FLAVOR

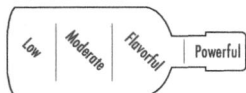

Low | Moderate | Flavorful | Powerful

3. PEATY

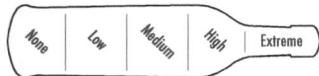

None | Low | Medium | High | Extreme

4. BODY

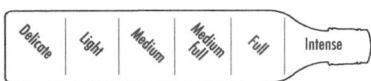

Delicate | Light | Medium | Medium Full | Full | Intense

5. SWEETNESS

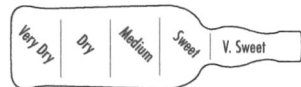

Very Dry | Dry | Medium | Sweet | V. Sweet

DOODLES & NOTES

6. FLAVOR GRAPH

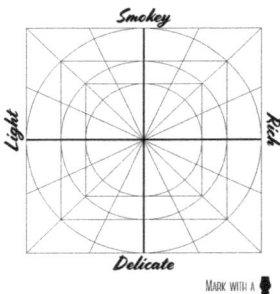

Smokey
Light
Rich
Delicate

MARK WITH A 🍾

7. FINISH

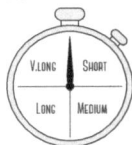

V. LONG | SHORT
LONG | MEDIUM

Describe it

8. BALANCE

Not Balanced | Balanced | Harmonious | Complex

9. DEPTH

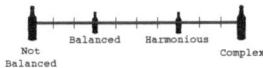

None | Medium | Great

10. OFF-FLAVORS?

OTHER THOUGHTS - What did you think of this one?

BOTTLE & LABEL

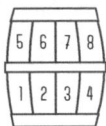

5 | 6 | 7 | 8
1 | 2 | 3 | 4

VALUE

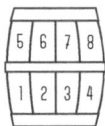

5 | 6 | 7 | 8
1 | 2 | 3 | 4

PRICE

DRINK AGAIN?

DESCRIBE IN 3 WORDS

_____
_____
_____

Distillery _____ Region _____

Whiskey Name _____ Country _____

Type _____ ABV _____

Age _____ Unicorn? 👍 Rating ⟨⟩ ⟨⟩ ⟨⟩ ⟨⟩ ⟨⟩

APPEARANCE – First, fill your glass! (Or draw your own)

| Swirling Glass | Vinum Single Malt | Large Glencairn | NEAT Glass | Wine | Glencairn | Straight Tumbler | Bourbon Tumbler | Draw Your Own! |

Now, hold it up against a white background. Describe what you see

1. CLARITY

Watery, Pale   Medium   Opaque, Deep

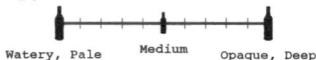

2. VISCOSITY / LEGS

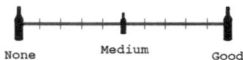

None   Medium   Good

3. COLOR & HUE

Lighter
Gold/Amber
Darker

Gin Clear	Pale Straw	Light Gold
Yellow Gold	Golden	Pale Amber
Rich Amber	Burnt Amber	Tawny
Mahogany	Old Oak	Treacle

4. DOODLES & NOTES

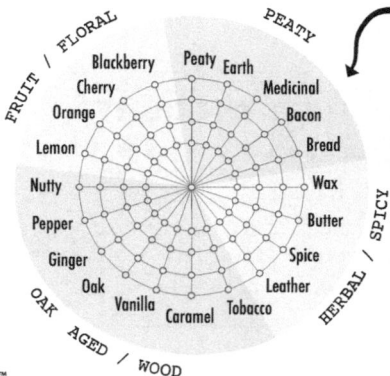

AROMA – Let's get your nose involved. Use the Aroma Wheel.

DOODLES & NOTES

Aroma Wheel: FRUIT / FLORAL, PEATY, HERBAL / SPICY, OAK AGED / WOOD

Blackberry, Cherry, Orange, Lemon, Nutty, Pepper, Ginger, Oak, Vanilla, Caramel, Tobacco, Leather, Spice, Butter, Wax, Bread, Bacon, Medicinal, Earth, Peaty

THE WHISKEY TASTING DOODLE BOOK™

TASTE - OK, now take a sip. Roll it around. Describe it.

1. FIRST TASTE

Clean | Sweet | Sour | Salty | Bitter

2. FLAVOR

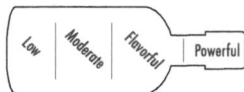

Low | Moderate | Flavorful | Powerful

3. PEATY

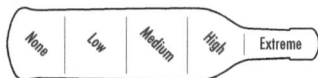

None | Low | Medium | High | Extreme

4. BODY

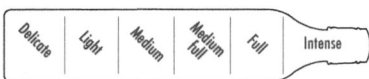

Delicate | Light | Medium | Medium full | Full | Intense

5. SWEETNESS

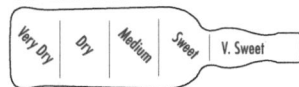

Very Dry | Dry | Medium | Sweet | V. Sweet

DOODLES & NOTES

6. FLAVOR GRAPH

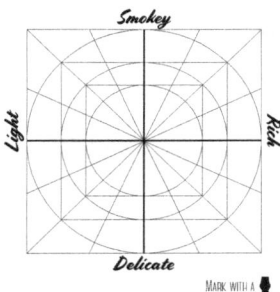

Smokey

Light

Rich

Delicate

MARK WITH A 🍸

7. FINISH

V.Long | Short | Long | Medium

Describe it

8. BALANCE

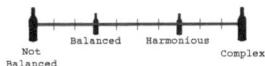

Not Balanced | Balanced | Harmonious | Complex

9. DEPTH

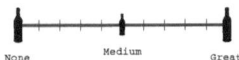

None | Medium | Great

10. OFF-FLAVORS?

OTHER THOUGHTS - What did you think of this one?

BOTTLE & LABEL

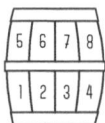

5 | 6 | 7 | 8
1 | 2 | 3 | 4

VALUE

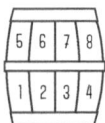

5 | 6 | 7 | 8
1 | 2 | 3 | 4

DRINK AGAIN?

PRICE

DESCRIBE IN 3 WORDS

_____

_____

_____

Distillery _____	Region _____
Whiskey Name _____	Country _____
Type _____	ABV _____
Age _____	Unicorn? 👍	Rating ▽▽▽▽▽

APPEARANCE - First, fill your glass! (Or draw your own)

Swirling Glass   Vinum Single Malt   Large Glencairn   NEAT Glass   Wine   Glencairn   Straight Tumbler   Bourbon Tumbler   Draw Your Own!

Now, hold it up against a white background. Describe what you see.

1. CLARITY

Watery, Pale   Medium   Opaque, Deep

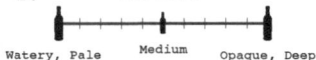

2. VISCOSITY / LEGS

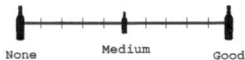

None   Medium   Good

3. COLOR & HUE

Lighter
Gold/Amber
Darker

Gin Clear	Pale Straw	Light Gold
Yellow Gold	Golden	Pale Amber
Rich Amber	Burnt Amber	Tawny
Mahogany	Old Oak	Treacle

4. DOODLES & NOTES

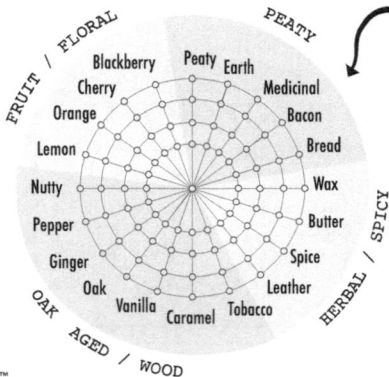

AROMA - Let's get your nose involved. Use the Aroma Wheel.

DOODLES & NOTES

FRUIT / FLORAL — Blackberry, Cherry, Orange, Lemon, Nutty, Pepper, Ginger

PEATY — Peaty, Earth, Medicinal, Bacon, Bread, Wax

HERBAL / SPICY — Butter, Spice, Leather, Tobacco

OAK AGED / WOOD — Oak, Vanilla, Caramel

THE WHISKEY TASTING DOODLE BOOK™

TASTE - OK, now take a sip. Roll it around. Describe it.

1. FIRST TASTE

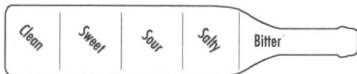

Clean | Sweet | Sour | Salty | Bitter

2. FLAVOR

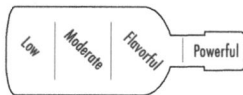

Low | Moderate | Flavorful | Powerful

3. PEATY

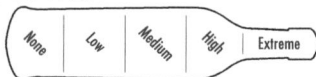

None | Low | Medium | High | Extreme

4. BODY

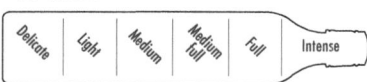

Delicate | Light | Medium | Medium full | Full | Intense

5. SWEETNESS

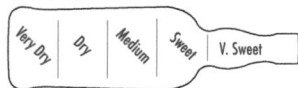

Very Dry | Dry | Medium | Sweet | V. Sweet

DOODLES & NOTES

6. FLAVOR GRAPH

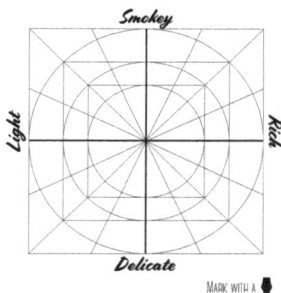

Smokey · Light · Rich · Delicate

MARK WITH A ●

7. FINISH

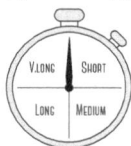

V.LONG | SHORT | LONG | MEDIUM

Describe it

8. BALANCE

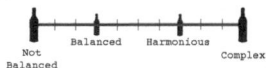

Not Balanced | Balanced | Harmonious | Complex

9. DEPTH

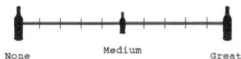

None | Medium | Great

10. OFF-FLAVORS?

OTHER THOUGHTS - What did you think of this one?

BOTTLE & LABEL

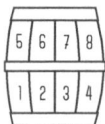

5 | 6 | 7 | 8
1 | 2 | 3 | 4

VALUE

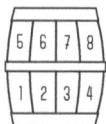

5 | 6 | 7 | 8
1 | 2 | 3 | 4

PRICE

DRINK AGAIN?

DESCRIBE IN 3 WORDS

_____
_____
_____

THE WHISKEY TASTING DOODLE BOOK™

LOG:

Distillery _____   Region _____

Whiskey Name _____   Country _____

Type _____   ABV _____

Age _____   Unicorn? 👍   Rating 🥃 🥃 🥃 🥃 🥃

APPEARANCE - First, fill your glass! (Or draw your own)

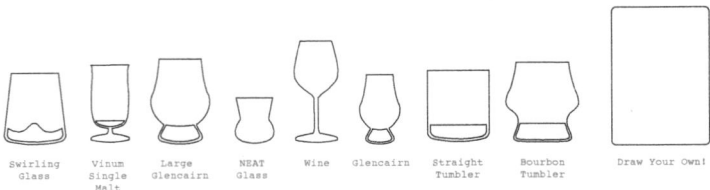

Swirling Glass | Vinum Single Malt | Large Glencairn | NEAT Glass | Wine | Glencairn | Straight Tumbler | Bourbon Tumbler | Draw Your Own!

Now, hold it up against a white background. Describe what you see

1. CLARITY

Watery, Pale — Medium — Opaque, Deep

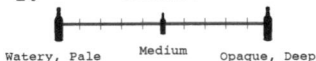

2. VISCOSITY / LEGS

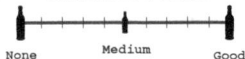

None — Medium — Good

3. COLOR & HUE

Lighter / Gold/Amber / Darker

Gin Clear	Pale Straw	Light Gold
Yellow Gold	Golden	Pale Amber
Rich Amber	Burnt Amber	Tawny
Mahogany	Old Oak	Treacle

4. DOODLES & NOTES

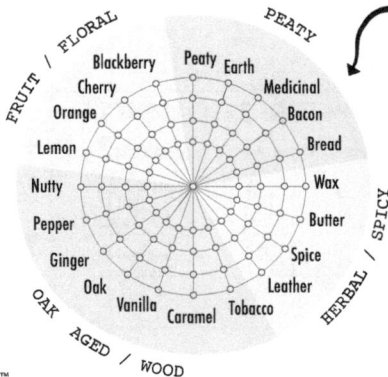

AROMA - Let's get your nose involved. Use the Aroma Wheel.

DOODLES & NOTES

FRUIT / FLORAL — PEATY — HERBAL / SPICY — OAK AGED / WOOD

Blackberry, Cherry, Orange, Lemon, Nutty, Pepper, Ginger, Oak, Vanilla, Caramel, Tobacco, Leather, Spice, Butter, Wax, Bread, Bacon, Medicinal, Earth, Peaty

THE WHISKEY TASTING DOODLE BOOK™

TASTE - OK, now take a sip. Roll it around. Describe it.

1. FIRST TASTE

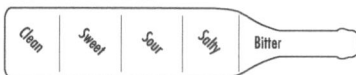

Clean | Sweet | Sour | Salty | Bitter

2. FLAVOR

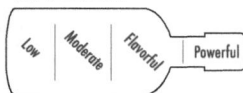

Low | Moderate | Flavorful | Powerful

3. PEATY

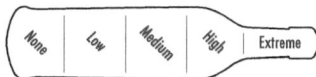

None | Low | Medium | High | Extreme

4. BODY

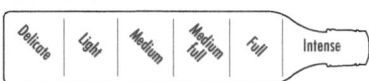

Delicate | Light | Medium | Medium Full | Full | Intense

5. SWEETNESS

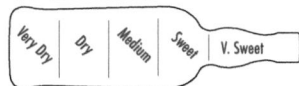

Very Dry | Dry | Medium | Sweet | V. Sweet

DOODLES & NOTES

6. FLAVOR GRAPH

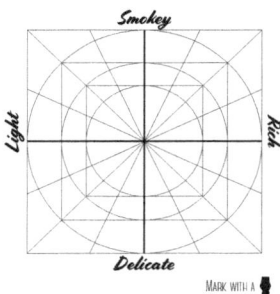

Smokey

Light

Rich

Delicate

MARK WITH A 🍸

7. FINISH

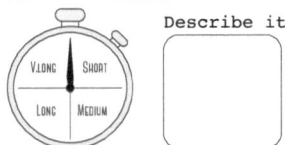

V. Long | Short | Long | Medium

Describe it

8. BALANCE

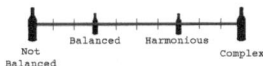

Not Balanced | Balanced | Harmonious | Complex

9. DEPTH

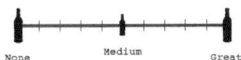

None | Medium | Great

10. OFF-FLAVORS?

OTHER THOUGHTS - What did you think of this one?

BOTTLE & LABEL

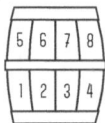

5 6 7 8
1 2 3 4

VALUE

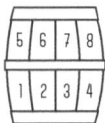

5 6 7 8
1 2 3 4

PRICE

DRINK AGAIN?

DESCRIBE IN 3 WORDS

_____
_____
_____

THE WHISKEY TASTING DOODLE BOOK™

LOG:

Distillery _____	Region _____
Whiskey Name _____	Country _____
Type _____	ABV _____
Age _____ Unicorn? 👍	Rating 🥃🥃🥃🥃🥃

APPEARANCE - First, fill your glass! (Or draw your own)

Swirling Glass   Vinum Single Malt   Large Glencairn   NEAT Glass   Wine   Glencairn   Straight Tumbler   Bourbon Tumbler   Draw Your Own!

Now, hold it up against a white background. Describe what you see

1. CLARITY

Watery, Pale — Medium — Opaque, Deep

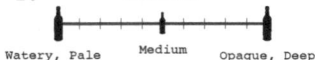

2. VISCOSITY / LEGS

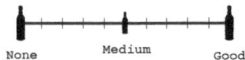

None — Medium — Good

3. COLOR & HUE

Lighter / *Gold/Amber* / *Darker*

Gin Clear	Pale Straw	Light Gold
Yellow Gold	Golden	Pale Amber
Rich Amber	Burnt Amber	Tawny
Mahogany	Old Oak	Treacle

4. DOODLES & NOTES

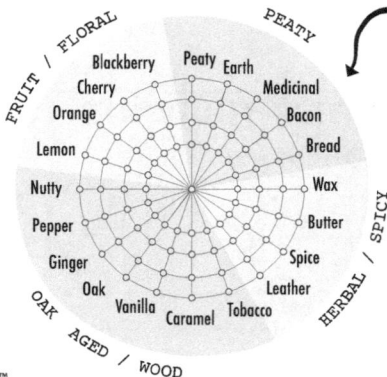

AROMA - Let's get your nose involved. Use the Aroma Wheel.

DOODLES & NOTES

Aroma Wheel:
FRUIT / FLORAL — Blackberry, Cherry, Orange, Lemon, Nutty, Pepper, Ginger
PEATY — Peaty, Earth, Medicinal, Bacon, Bread
SPICY — Wax, Butter, Spice, Leather
HERBAL / SPICY — Tobacco
OAK AGED / WOOD — Oak, Vanilla, Caramel

THE WHISKEY TASTING DOODLE BOOK™

TASTE - OK, now take a sip. Roll it around. Describe it.

1. FIRST TASTE

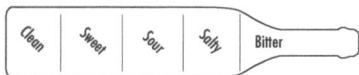

Clean | Sweet | Sour | Salty | Bitter

2. FLAVOR

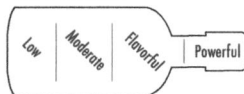

Low | Moderate | Flavorful | Powerful

3. PEATY

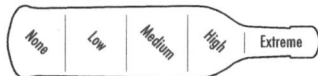

None | Low | Medium | High | Extreme

4. BODY

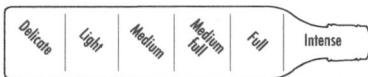

Delicate | Light | Medium | Medium full | Full | Intense

5. SWEETNESS

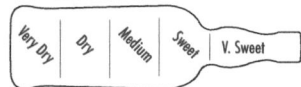

Very Dry | Dry | Medium | Sweet | V. Sweet

DOODLES & NOTES

6. FLAVOR GRAPH

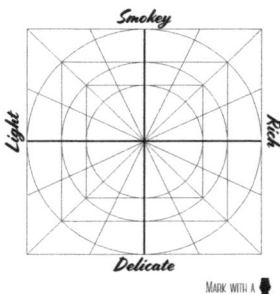

Smokey

Light

Rich

Delicate

MARK WITH A ⬛

7. FINISH

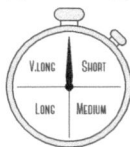

V. LONG | SHORT
LONG | MEDIUM

Describe it

8. BALANCE

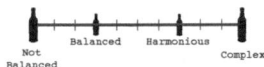

Not Balanced | Balanced | Harmonious | Complex

9. DEPTH

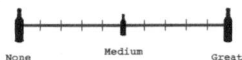

None | Medium | Great

10. OFF-FLAVORS?

OTHER THOUGHTS - What did you think of this one?

BOTTLE & LABEL

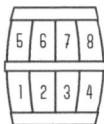

5 | 6 | 7 | 8
1 | 2 | 3 | 4

VALUE

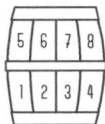

5 | 6 | 7 | 8
1 | 2 | 3 | 4

PRICE

DRINK AGAIN?

DESCRIBE IN 3 WORDS

Distillery _____	Region _____
Whiskey Name _____	Country _____
Type _____	ABV _____
Age _____	Unicorn? 👍	Rating ♢♢♢♢♢

APPEARANCE - First, fill your glass! (Or draw your own)

Swirling Glass · Vinum Single Malt · Large Glencairn · NEAT Glass · Wine · Glencairn · Straight Tumbler · Bourbon Tumbler · Draw Your Own!

Now, hold it up against a white background. Describe what you see.

1. CLARITY

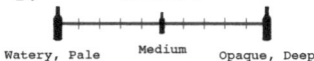

Watery, Pale — Medium — Opaque, Deep

2. VISCOSITY / LEGS

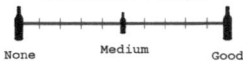

None — Medium — Good

3. COLOR & HUE

Lighter
Gold/Amber
Darker

Gin Clear · Pale Straw · Light Gold
Yellow Gold · Golden · Pale Amber
Rich Amber · Burnt Amber · Tawny
Mahogany · Old Oak · Treacle

4. DOODLES & NOTES

AROMA - Let's get your nose involved. Use the Aroma Wheel.

DOODLES & NOTES

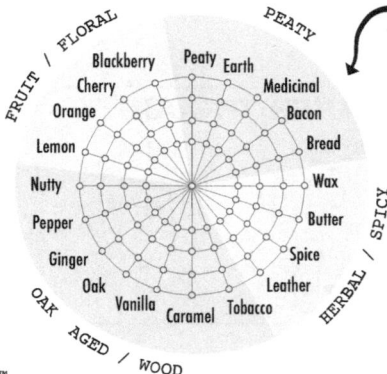

FRUIT / FLORAL · PEATY · HERBAL / SPICY · OAK AGED / WOOD

Blackberry · Cherry · Orange · Lemon · Nutty · Pepper · Ginger · Oak · Vanilla · Caramel · Tobacco · Leather · Spice · Butter · Wax · Bread · Bacon · Medicinal · Earth · Peaty

THE WHISKEY TASTING DOODLE BOOK™

TASTE - OK, now take a sip. Roll it around. Describe it.

1. FIRST TASTE

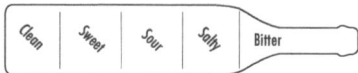

Clean | Sweet | Sour | Salty | Bitter

2. FLAVOR

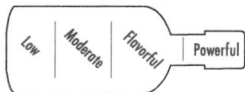

Low | Moderate | Flavorful | Powerful

3. PEATY

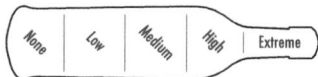

None | Low | Medium | High | Extreme

4. BODY

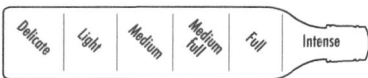

Delicate | Light | Medium | Medium full | Full | Intense

5. SWEETNESS

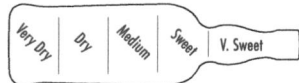

Very Dry | Dry | Medium | Sweet | V. Sweet

DOODLES & NOTES

6. FLAVOR GRAPH

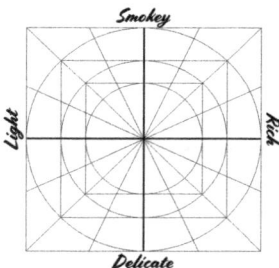

Smokey

Light

Rich

Delicate

MARK WITH A ⬇

7. FINISH

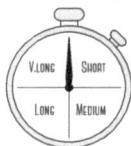

V.LONG | SHORT
LONG | MEDIUM

Describe it

8. BALANCE

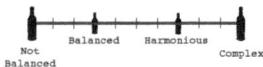

Not Balanced | Balanced | Harmonious | Complex

9. DEPTH

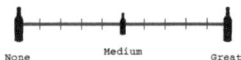

None | Medium | Great

10. OFF-FLAVORS?

OTHER THOUGHTS - What did you think of this one?

BOTTLE & LABEL

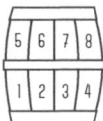

5 6 7 8
1 2 3 4

VALUE

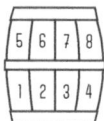

5 6 7 8
1 2 3 4

PRICE

DRINK AGAIN?

DESCRIBE IN 3 WORDS

_____
_____
_____

LOG:

Distillery _____   Region _____

Whiskey Name _____   Country _____

Type _____   ABV _____

Age _____   Unicorn? 👍   Rating 🥃🥃🥃🥃🥃

APPEARANCE – First, fill your glass! (Or draw your own)

Swirling Glass | Vinum Single Malt | Large Glencairn | NEAT Glass | Wine | Glencairn | Straight Tumbler | Bourbon Tumbler | Draw Your Own!

Now, hold it up against a white background. Describe what you see.

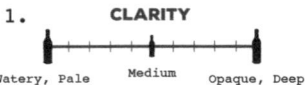

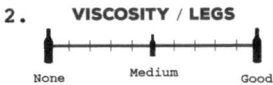

1. CLARITY

Watery, Pale — Medium — Opaque, Deep

2. VISCOSITY / LEGS

None — Medium — Good

3. COLOR & HUE

Lighter
ld/Amber
Darker

Gin Clear	Pale Straw	Light Gold
Yellow Gold	Golden	Pale Amber
Rich Amber	Burnt Amber	Tawny
Mahogany	Old Oak	Treacle

4. DOODLES & NOTES

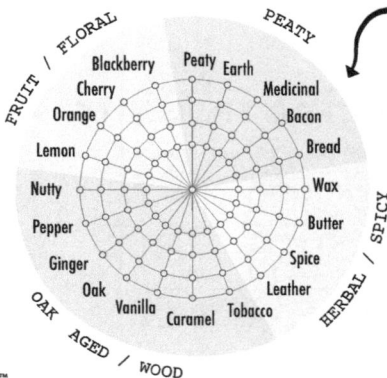

AROMA – Let's get your nose involved. Use the Aroma Wheel.

DOODLES & NOTES

FRUIT / FLORAL — PEATY

Blackberry, Cherry, Orange, Lemon, Nutty, Pepper, Ginger, Oak

Peaty, Earth, Medicinal, Bacon, Bread, Wax, Butter, Spice, Leather, Tobacco

Vanilla, Caramel

OAK AGED / WOOD — HERBAL / SPICY

THE WHISKEY TASTING DOODLE BOOK™

TASTE - OK, now take a sip. Roll it around. Describe it.

1. FIRST TASTE

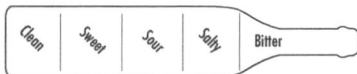

Clean | Sweet | Sour | Salty | Bitter

2. FLAVOR

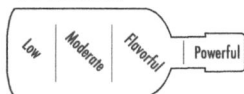

Low | Moderate | Flavorful | Powerful

3. PEATY

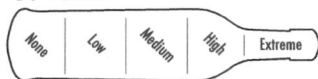

None | Low | Medium | High | Extreme

4. BODY

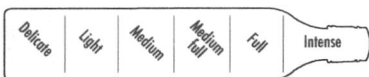

Delicate | Light | Medium | Medium Full | Full | Intense

5. SWEETNESS

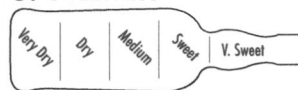

Very Dry | Dry | Medium | Sweet | V. Sweet

DOODLES & NOTES

6. FLAVOR GRAPH

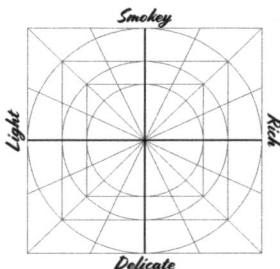

Smokey

Light

Rich

Delicate

MARK WITH A 🍶

7. FINISH

V. LONG | SHORT
LONG | MEDIUM

Describe it

8. BALANCE

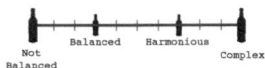

Not Balanced | Balanced | Harmonious | Complex

9. DEPTH

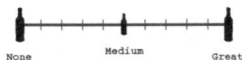

None | Medium | Great

10. OFF-FLAVORS?

OTHER THOUGHTS - What did you think of this one?

BOTTLE & LABEL

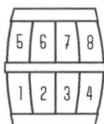

5 | 6 | 7 | 8
1 | 2 | 3 | 4

VALUE

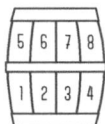

5 | 6 | 7 | 8
1 | 2 | 3 | 4

PRICE

DRINK AGAIN?

DESCRIBE IN 3 WORDS

LOG:

Distillery _____ Region _____

Whiskey Name _____ Country _____

Type _____ ABV _____

Age _____ Unicorn? 👍 Rating 🥃 🥃 🥃 🥃 🥃

APPEARANCE - First, fill your glass! (Or draw your own)

Swirling Glass | Vinum Single Malt | Large Glencairn | NEAT Glass | Wine | Glencairn | Straight Tumbler | Bourbon Tumbler | Draw Your Own!

Now, hold it up against a white background. Describe what you see.

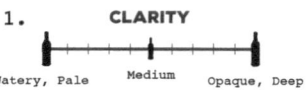

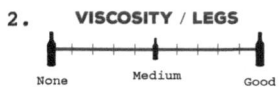

1. CLARITY

Watery, Pale   Medium   Opaque, Deep

2. VISCOSITY / LEGS

None   Medium   Good

3. COLOR & HUE

Lighter | Gin Clear | Pale Straw | Light Gold
Gold/Amber | Yellow Gold | Golden | Pale Amber
| Rich Amber | Burnt Amber | Tawny
Darker | Mahogany | Old Oak | Treacle

4. DOODLES & NOTES

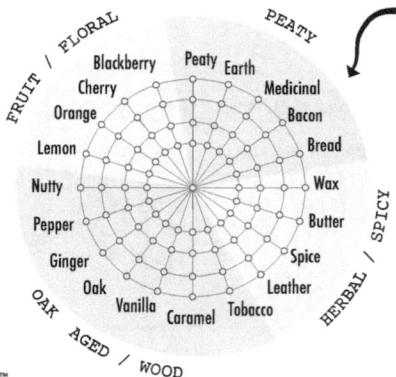

AROMA - Let's get your nose involved. Use the Aroma Wheel.

DOODLES & NOTES

FRUIT / FLORAL — PEATY — HERBAL / SPICY — OAK AGED / WOOD

Blackberry, Cherry, Orange, Lemon, Nutty, Pepper, Ginger, Oak, Vanilla, Caramel, Tobacco, Leather, Spice, Butter, Wax, Bread, Bacon, Medicinal, Earth, Peaty

THE WHISKEY TASTING DOODLE BOOK™

TASTE - OK, now take a sip. Roll it around. Describe it.

1. FIRST TASTE

Clean | Sweet | Sour | Salty | Bitter

2. FLAVOR

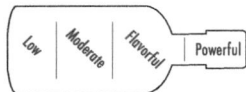

Low | Moderate | Flavorful | Powerful

3. PEATY

None | Low | Medium | High | Extreme

4. BODY

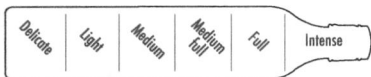

Delicate | Light | Medium | Medium Full | Full | Intense

5. SWEETNESS

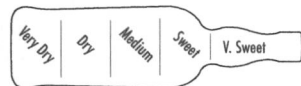

Very Dry | Dry | Medium | Sweet | V. Sweet

DOODLES & NOTES

6. FLAVOR GRAPH

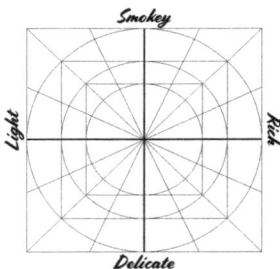

Smokey

Light

Rich

Delicate

MARK WITH A ●

7. FINISH

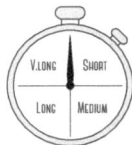

V. LONG | SHORT | LONG | MEDIUM

Describe it

8. BALANCE

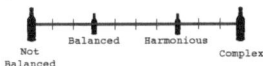

Not Balanced | Balanced | Harmonious | Complex

9. DEPTH

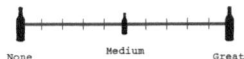

None | Medium | Great

10. OFF-FLAVORS?

OTHER THOUGHTS - What did you think of this one?

BOTTLE & LABEL

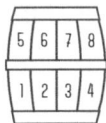

5 | 6 | 7 | 8
1 | 2 | 3 | 4

VALUE

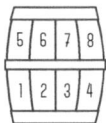

5 | 6 | 7 | 8
1 | 2 | 3 | 4

PRICE

DRINK AGAIN?

DESCRIBE IN 3 WORDS

_____
_____
_____

THE WHISKEY TASTING DOODLE BOOK™

LOG:

Distillery _____   Region _____

Whiskey Name _____   Country _____

Type _____   ABV _____

Age _____   Unicorn? 👍   Rating 🥃🥃🥃🥃🥃

APPEARANCE – First, fill your glass! (Or draw your own)

| Swirling Glass | Vinum Single Malt | Large Glencairn | NEAT Glass | Wine | Glencairn | Straight Tumbler | Bourbon Tumbler | Draw Your Own! |

Now, hold it up against a white background. Describe what you see

1. CLARITY

Watery, Pale — Medium — Opaque, Deep

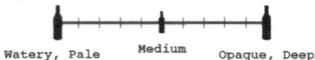

2. VISCOSITY / LEGS

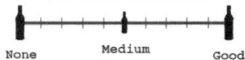

None — Medium — Good

3. COLOR & HUE

Lighter / Gold/Amber / Darker

Gin Clear	Pale Straw	Light Gold
Yellow Gold	Golden	Pale Amber
Rich Amber	Burnt Amber	Tawny
Mahogany	Old Oak	Treacle

4. DOODLES & NOTES

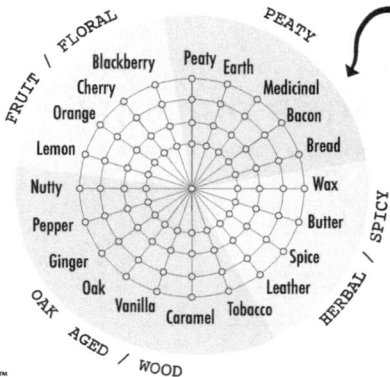

AROMA – Let's get your nose involved. Use the Aroma Wheel.

DOODLES & NOTES

Aroma wheel with the following labels:

FRUIT / FLORAL — PEATY — HERBAL / SPICY — OAK AGED / WOOD

Blackberry, Cherry, Orange, Lemon, Nutty, Pepper, Ginger, Oak, Vanilla, Caramel, Tobacco, Leather, Spice, Butter, Wax, Bread, Bacon, Medicinal, Earth, Peaty

THE WHISKEY TASTING DOODLE BOOK™

TASTE - OK, now take a sip. Roll it around. Describe it.

1. FIRST TASTE

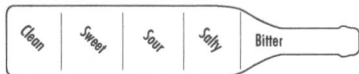

Clean | Sweet | Sour | Salty | Bitter

2. FLAVOR

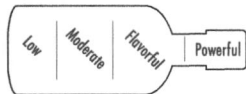

Low | Moderate | Flavorful | Powerful

3. PEATY

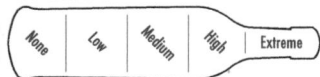

None | Low | Medium | High | Extreme

4. BODY

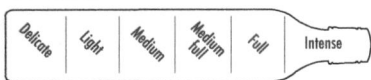

Delicate | Light | Medium | Medium Full | Full | Intense

5. SWEETNESS

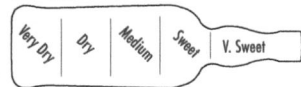

Very Dry | Dry | Medium | Sweet | V. Sweet

DOODLES & NOTES

6. FLAVOR GRAPH

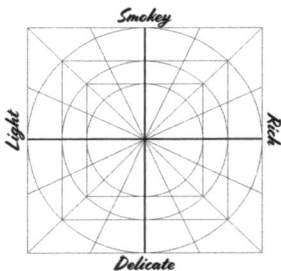

Smokey

Light

Rich

Delicate

MARK WITH A 🍶

7. FINISH

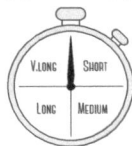

V.LONG | SHORT
LONG | MEDIUM

Describe it

8. BALANCE

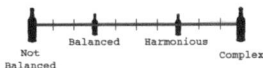

Not Balanced | Balanced | Harmonious | Complex

9. DEPTH

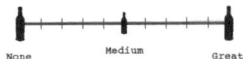

None | Medium | Great

10. OFF-FLAVORS?

OTHER THOUGHTS - What did you think of this one?

BOTTLE & LABEL

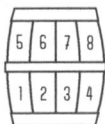

5 | 6 | 7 | 8
1 | 2 | 3 | 4

VALUE

5 | 6 | 7 | 8
1 | 2 | 3 | 4

PRICE

DRINK AGAIN?

DESCRIBE IN 3 WORDS

_____
_____
_____

LOG:

Distillery _____	Region _____
Whiskey Name _____	Country _____
Type _____	ABV _____
Age _____ Unicorn? 👍	Rating 🥃🥃🥃🥃🥃

APPEARANCE - First, fill your glass! (Or draw your own)

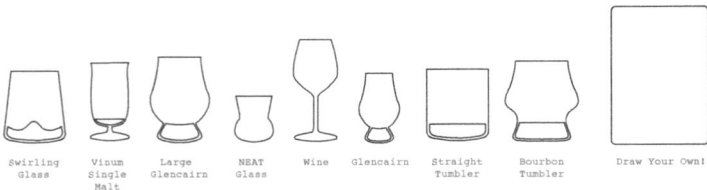

Swirling Glass · Vinum Single Malt · Large Glencairn · NEAT Glass · Wine · Glencairn · Straight Tumbler · Bourbon Tumbler · Draw Your Own!

Now, hold it up against a white background. Describe what you see

1. CLARITY

Watery, Pale — Medium — Opaque, Deep

2. VISCOSITY / LEGS

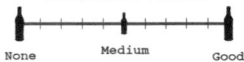

None — Medium — Good

3. COLOR & HUE

Lighter Gold/Amber Darker

Gin Clear	Pale Straw	Light Gold
Yellow Gold	Golden	Pale Amber
Rich Amber	Burnt Amber	Tawny
Mahogany	Old Oak	Treacle

4. DOODLES & NOTES

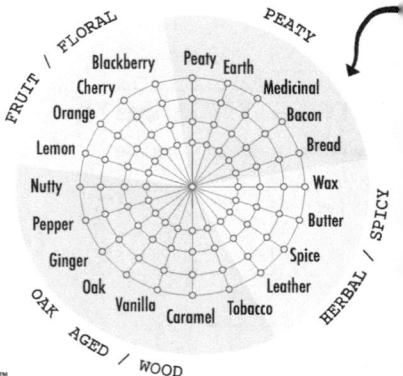

AROMA - Let's get your nose involved. Use the Aroma Wheel.

DOODLES & NOTES

FRUIT / FLORAL — PEATY
Blackberry, Cherry, Orange, Lemon, Nutty, Pepper, Ginger, Oak, Vanilla, Caramel, Tobacco, Leather, Spice, Butter, Wax, Bread, Bacon, Medicinal, Peaty, Earth
OAK AGED / WOOD — HERBAL / SPICY

THE WHISKEY TASTING DOODLE BOOK™

TASTE - OK, now take a sip. Roll it around. Describe it.

1. FIRST TASTE
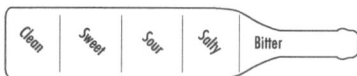
Clean | Sweet | Sour | Salty | Bitter

2. FLAVOR
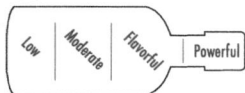
Low | Moderate | Flavorful | Powerful

3. PEATY

None | Low | Medium | High | Extreme

4. BODY

Delicate | Light | Medium | Medium full | Full | Intense

5. SWEETNESS
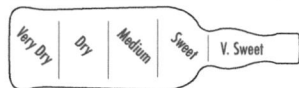
Very Dry | Dry | Medium | Sweet | V. Sweet

DOODLES & NOTES

6. FLAVOR GRAPH
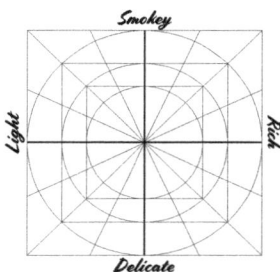
Smokey | Light | Rich | Delicate

MARK WITH A ●

7. FINISH
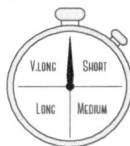
V.LONG | SHORT | LONG | MEDIUM

Describe it

8. BALANCE
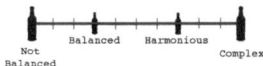
Not Balanced | Balanced | Harmonious | Complex

9. DEPTH
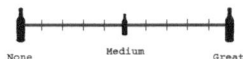
None | Medium | Great

10. OFF-FLAVORS?

OTHER THOUGHTS - What did you think of this one?

BOTTLE & LABEL
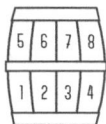
5 | 6 | 7 | 8
1 | 2 | 3 | 4

VALUE
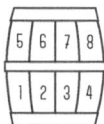
5 | 6 | 7 | 8
1 | 2 | 3 | 4

PRICE

DRINK AGAIN?

DESCRIBE IN 3 WORDS

Distillery _____ Region _____

Whiskey Name _____ Country _____

Type _____ ABV _____

Age _____ Unicorn? 👍 Rating 🥃🥃🥃🥃🥃

APPEARANCE – First, fill your glass! (Or draw your own)

| Swirling Glass | Vinum Single Malt | Large Glencairn | NEAT Glass | Wine | Glencairn | Straight Tumbler | Bourbon Tumbler | Draw Your Own! |

Now, hold it up against a white background. Describe what you see

1. CLARITY

Watery, Pale — Medium — Opaque, Deep

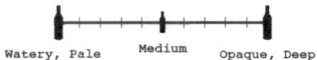

2. VISCOSITY / LEGS

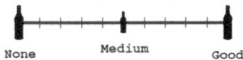

None — Medium — Good

3. COLOR & HUE

Lighter Gold/Amber Darker

Gin Clear	Pale Straw	Light Gold
Yellow Gold	Golden	Pale Amber
Rich Amber	Burnt Amber	Tawny
Mahogany	Old Oak	Treacle

4. DOODLES & NOTES

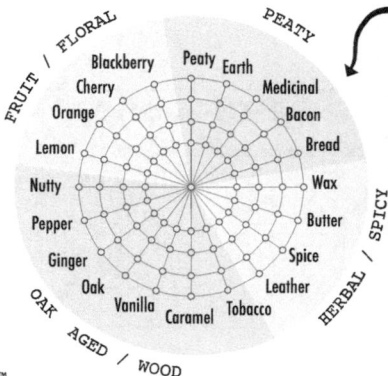

AROMA – Let's get your nose involved. Use the Aroma Wheel.

DOODLES & NOTES

FRUIT / FLORAL — PEATY — HERBAL / SPICY — OAK AGED / WOOD

Blackberry, Cherry, Orange, Lemon, Nutty, Pepper, Ginger, Oak, Vanilla, Caramel, Tobacco, Leather, Spice, Butter, Wax, Bread, Bacon, Medicinal, Earth, Peaty

THE WHISKEY TASTING DOODLE BOOK™

TASTE - OK, now take a sip. Roll it around. Describe it.

1. FIRST TASTE
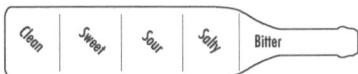
Clean | Sweet | Sour | Salty | Bitter

2. FLAVOR
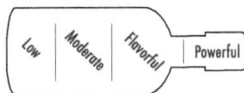
Low | Moderate | Flavorful | Powerful

3. PEATY

None | Low | Medium | High | Extreme

4. BODY

Delicate | Light | Medium | Medium Full | Full | Intense

5. SWEETNESS
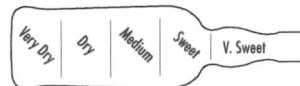
Very Dry | Dry | Medium | Sweet | V. Sweet

DOODLES & NOTES

6. FLAVOR GRAPH
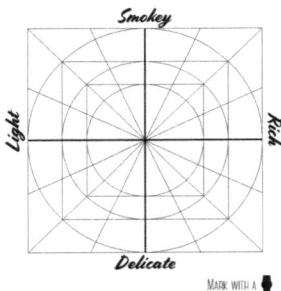
Smokey / Light / Rich / Delicate
MARK WITH A

7. FINISH
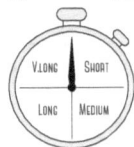
V. Long | Short | Long | Medium

Describe it

8. BALANCE
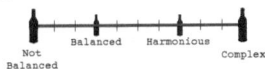
Not Balanced | Balanced | Harmonious | Complex

9. DEPTH
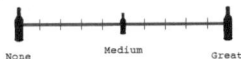
None | Medium | Great

10. OFF-FLAVORS?

OTHER THOUGHTS - What did you think of this one?

BOTTLE & LABEL
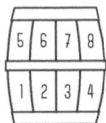
5 6 7 8
1 2 3 4

VALUE
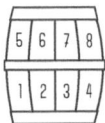
5 6 7 8
1 2 3 4

PRICE

DRINK AGAIN?

DESCRIBE IN 3 WORDS

LOG:

Distillery _____   Region _____

Whiskey Name _____   Country _____

Type _____   ABV _____

Age _____ Unicorn? 👍 Rating ⬡⬡⬡⬡⬡

APPEARANCE – First, fill your glass! (Or draw your own)

Swirling Glass | Vinum Single Malt | Large Glencairn | NEAT Glass | Wine | Glencairn | Straight Tumbler | Bourbon Tumbler | Draw Your Own!

Now, hold it up against a white background. Describe what you see.

1. CLARITY

Watery, Pale   Medium   Opaque, Deep

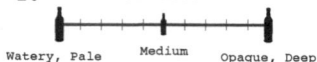

2. VISCOSITY / LEGS

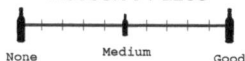

None   Medium   Good

3. COLOR & HUE

Lighter
ld/Amber
Darker

Gin Clear	Pale Straw	Light Gold
Yellow Gold	Golden	Pale Amber
Rich Amber	Burnt Amber	Tawny
Mahogany	Old Oak	Treacle

4. DOODLES & NOTES

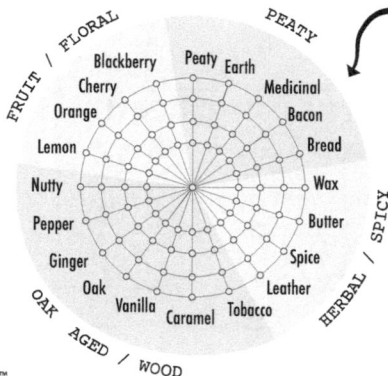

AROMA – Let's get your nose involved. Use the Aroma Wheel.

DOODLES & NOTES

FRUIT / FLORAL — PEATY — SPICY — HERBAL / SPICY — OAK AGED / WOOD

Blackberry, Cherry, Orange, Lemon, Nutty, Pepper, Ginger, Oak, Vanilla, Caramel, Tobacco, Leather, Spice, Butter, Wax, Bread, Bacon, Medicinal, Earth, Peaty

TASTE - OK, now take a sip. Roll it around. Describe it.

1. FIRST TASTE

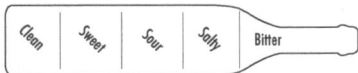

Clean | Sweet | Sour | Salty | Bitter

2. FLAVOR

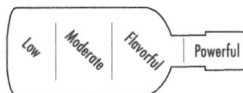

Low | Moderate | Flavorful | Powerful

3. PEATY

None | Low | Medium | High | Extreme

4. BODY

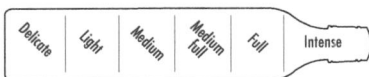

Delicate | Light | Medium | Medium full | Full | Intense

5. SWEETNESS

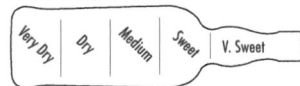

Very Dry | Dry | Medium | Sweet | V. Sweet

DOODLES & NOTES

6. FLAVOR GRAPH

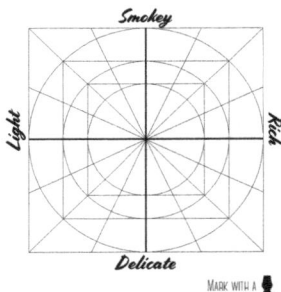

Smokey

Light

Rich

Delicate

MARK WITH A 🖤

7. FINISH

V. Long | Short | Long | Medium

Describe it

8. BALANCE

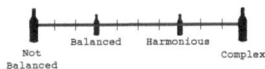

Not Balanced | Balanced | Harmonious | Complex

9. DEPTH

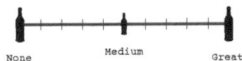

None | Medium | Great

10. OFF-FLAVORS?

OTHER THOUGHTS - What did you think of this one?

BOTTLE & LABEL

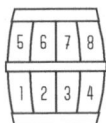

5 | 6 | 7 | 8
1 | 2 | 3 | 4

VALUE

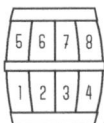

5 | 6 | 7 | 8
1 | 2 | 3 | 4

PRICE

DRINK AGAIN?

DESCRIBE IN 3 WORDS

LOG:

Distillery _____   Region _____

Whiskey Name _____   Country _____

Type _____   ABV _____

Age _____   Unicorn? 👍   Rating 🥃🥃🥃🥃🥃

APPEARANCE - First, fill your glass! (Or draw your own)

Swirling Glass   Vinum Single Malt   Large Glencairn   NEAT Glass   Wine   Glencairn   Straight Tumbler   Bourbon Tumbler   Draw Your Own!

Now, hold it up against a white background. Describe what you see

1. CLARITY

Watery, Pale   Medium   Opaque, Deep

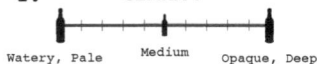

2. VISCOSITY / LEGS

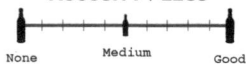

None   Medium   Good

3. COLOR & HUE

Lighter
Gold/Amber
Darker

Gin Clear	Pale Straw	Light Gold
Yellow Gold	Golden	Pale Amber
Rich Amber	Burnt Amber	Tawny
Mahogany	Old Oak	Treacle

4. DOODLES & NOTES

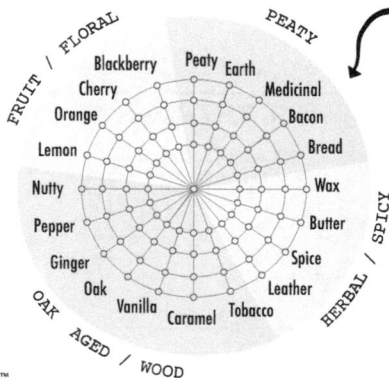

AROMA - Let's get your nose involved. Use the Aroma Wheel.

DOODLES & NOTES

FRUIT / FLORAL — PEATY — HERBAL / SPICY — OAK AGED / WOOD

Blackberry, Cherry, Orange, Lemon, Nutty, Pepper, Ginger, Oak, Vanilla, Caramel, Tobacco, Leather, Spice, Butter, Wax, Bread, Bacon, Medicinal, Earth, Peaty

THE WHISKEY TASTING DOODLE BOOK™

TASTE - OK, now take a sip. Roll it around. Describe it.

1. FIRST TASTE
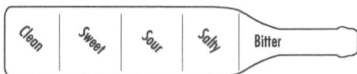
Clean | Sweet | Sour | Salty | Bitter

2. FLAVOR
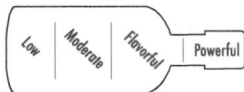
Low | Moderate | Flavorful | Powerful

3. PEATY
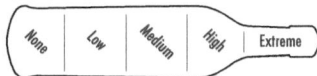
None | Low | Medium | High | Extreme

4. BODY
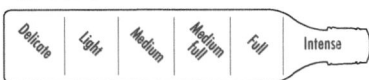
Delicate | Light | Medium | Medium full | Full | Intense

5. SWEETNESS
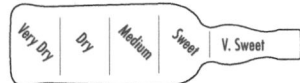
Very Dry | Dry | Medium | Sweet | V. Sweet

DOODLES & NOTES

6. FLAVOR GRAPH
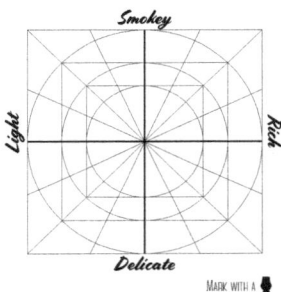
Smokey / Light / Rich / Delicate

MARK WITH A ●

7. FINISH
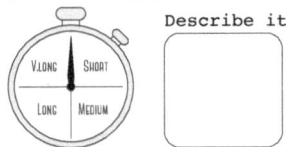
V. LONG | SHORT | LONG | MEDIUM

Describe it

8. BALANCE
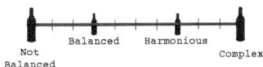
Not Balanced | Balanced | Harmonious | Complex

9. DEPTH
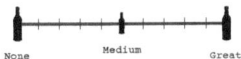
None | Medium | Great

10. OFF-FLAVORS?

OTHER THOUGHTS - What did you think of this one?

BOTTLE & LABEL
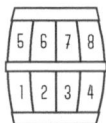
5 | 6 | 7 | 8
1 | 2 | 3 | 4

VALUE
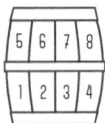
5 | 6 | 7 | 8
1 | 2 | 3 | 4

PRICE

DRINK AGAIN?

DESCRIBE IN 3 WORDS

THE WHISKEY TASTING DOODLE BOOK™

LOG:

Distillery _____   Region _____

Whiskey Name _____   Country _____

Type _____   ABV _____

Age _____   Unicorn? 👍   Rating 🥃 🥃 🥃 🥃 🥃

APPEARANCE - First, fill your glass! (Or draw your own)

Swirling Glass   Vinum Single Malt   Large Glencairn   NEAT Glass   Wine   Glencairn   Straight Tumbler   Bourbon Tumbler   Draw Your Own!

Now, hold it up against a white background. Describe what you see.

1. CLARITY

Watery, Pale   Medium   Opaque, Deep

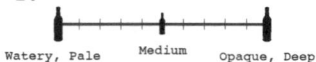

2. VISCOSITY / LEGS

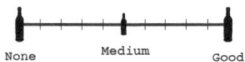

None   Medium   Good

3. COLOR & HUE

Lighter / Gold/Amber / Darker

Gin Clear	Pale Straw	Light Gold
Yellow Gold	Golden	Pale Amber
Rich Amber	Burnt Amber	Tawny
Mahogany	Old Oak	Treacle

4. DOODLES & NOTES

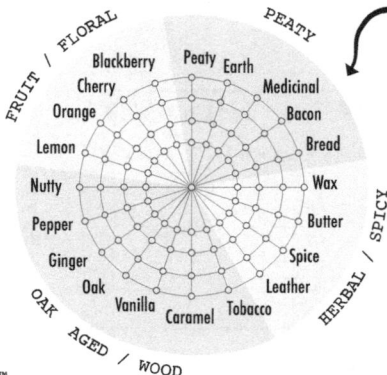

AROMA - Let's get your nose involved. Use the Aroma Wheel.

DOODLES & NOTES

FRUIT / FLORAL: Blackberry, Cherry, Orange, Lemon, Nutty, Pepper, Ginger

PEATY: Peaty, Earth, Medicinal, Bacon, Bread

HERBAL / SPICY: Wax, Butter, Spice, Leather

OAK AGED / WOOD: Oak, Vanilla, Caramel, Tobacco

THE WHISKEY TASTING DOODLE BOOK™

TASTE - OK, now take a sip. Roll it around. Describe it.

1. FIRST TASTE

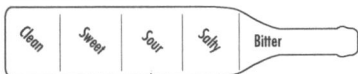

Clean | Sweet | Sour | Salty | Bitter

2. FLAVOR

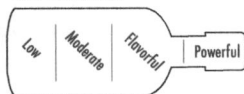

Low | Moderate | Flavorful | Powerful

3. PEATY

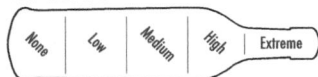

None | Low | Medium | High | Extreme

4. BODY

Delicate | Light | Medium | Medium Full | Full | Intense

5. SWEETNESS

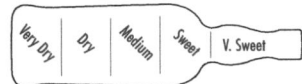

Very Dry | Dry | Medium | Sweet | V. Sweet

DOODLES & NOTES

6. FLAVOR GRAPH

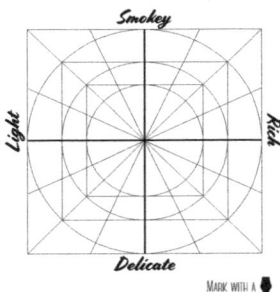

Smokey
Light
Rich
Delicate

MARK WITH A ♣

7. FINISH

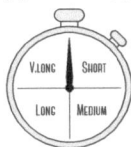

V. Long | Short | Long | Medium

Describe it

8. BALANCE

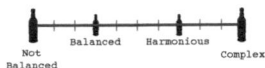

Not Balanced | Balanced | Harmonious | Complex

9. DEPTH

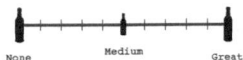

None | Medium | Great

10. OFF-FLAVORS?

OTHER THOUGHTS - What did you think of this one?

BOTTLE & LABEL

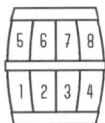

5 | 6 | 7 | 8
1 | 2 | 3 | 4

VALUE

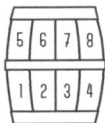

5 | 6 | 7 | 8
1 | 2 | 3 | 4

PRICE

DRINK AGAIN?

DESCRIBE IN 3 WORDS

LOG:

Distillery _____	Region _____
Whiskey Name _____	Country _____
Type _____	ABV _____
Age _____ Unicorn? 👍	Rating 🥃🥃🥃🥃🥃

APPEARANCE – First, fill your glass! (Or draw your own)

Swirling Glass | Vinum Single Malt | Large Glencairn | NEAT Glass | Wine | Glencairn | Straight Tumbler | Bourbon Tumbler | Draw Your Own!

Now, hold it up against a white background. Describe what you see.

1. CLARITY

Watery, Pale — Medium — Opaque, Deep

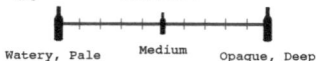

2. VISCOSITY / LEGS

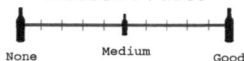

None — Medium — Good

3. COLOR & HUE

Lighter / ld/Amber / Darker

Gin Clear	Pale Straw	Light Gold
Yellow Gold	Golden	Pale Amber
Rich Amber	Burnt Amber	Tawny
Mahogany	Old Oak	Treacle

4. DOODLES & NOTES

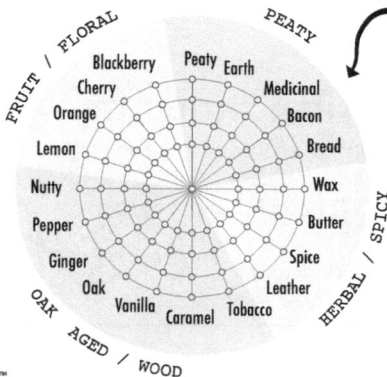

AROMA – Let's get your nose involved. Use the Aroma Wheel.

DOODLES & NOTES

FRUIT / FLORAL — PEATY

Blackberry, Cherry, Orange, Lemon, Nutty, Pepper, Ginger, Oak, Vanilla, Caramel, Tobacco, Leather, Spice, Butter, Wax, Bread, Bacon, Medicinal, Earth, Peaty

OAK AGED / WOOD — HERBAL / SPICY

THE WHISKEY TASTING DOODLE BOOK™

TASTE - OK, now take a sip. Roll it around. Describe it.

1. FIRST TASTE

Clean | Sweet | Sour | Salty | Bitter

2. FLAVOR

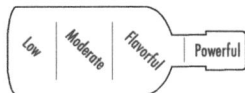

Low | Moderate | Flavorful | Powerful

3. PEATY

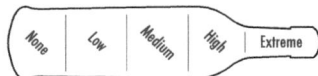

None | Low | Medium | High | Extreme

4. BODY

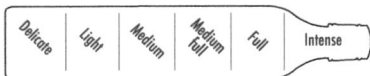

Delicate | Light | Medium | Medium full | Full | Intense

5. SWEETNESS

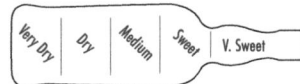

Very Dry | Dry | Medium | Sweet | V. Sweet

DOODLES & NOTES

6. FLAVOR GRAPH

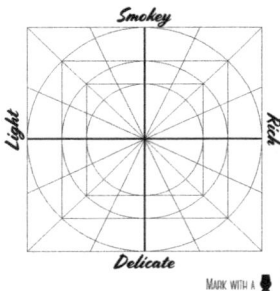

Smokey

Light

Rich

Delicate

MARK WITH A 🍶

7. FINISH

V.LONG | SHORT
LONG | MEDIUM

Describe it

8. BALANCE

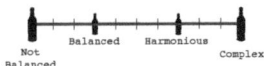

Not Balanced | Balanced | Harmonious | Complex

9. DEPTH

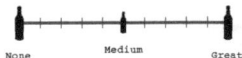

None | Medium | Great

10. OFF-FLAVORS?

OTHER THOUGHTS - What did you think of this one?

BOTTLE & LABEL

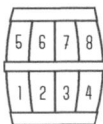

5 6 7 8
1 2 3 4

VALUE

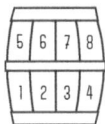

5 6 7 8
1 2 3 4

PRICE

DRINK AGAIN?

DESCRIBE IN 3 WORDS

____

____

____

THE WHISKEY TASTING DOODLE BOOK™

LOG:

Distillery _____	Region _____
Whiskey Name _____	Country _____
Type _____	ABV _____
Age _____ Unicorn? 👍	Rating 🥃🥃🥃🥃🥃

APPEARANCE - First, fill your glass! (Or draw your own)

Swirling Glass | Vinum Single Malt | Large Glencairn | NEAT Glass | Wine | Glencairn | Straight Tumbler | Bourbon Tumbler | Draw Your Own!

Now, hold it up against a white background. Describe what you see.

1. CLARITY

Watery, Pale — Medium — Opaque, Deep

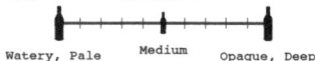

2. VISCOSITY / LEGS

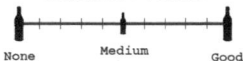

None — Medium — Good

3. COLOR & HUE

Lighter
ld/Amber
Darker

Gin Clear	Pale Straw	Light Gold
Yellow Gold	Golden	Pale Amber
Rich Amber	Burnt Amber	Tawny
Mahogany	Old Oak	Treacle

4. DOODLES & NOTES

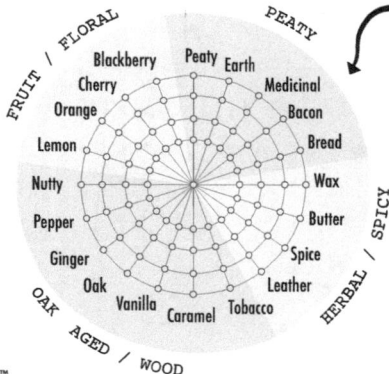

AROMA - Let's get your nose involved. Use the Aroma Wheel.

DOODLES & NOTES

Aroma Wheel: FRUIT / FLORAL, PEATY, HERBAL / SPICY, OAK AGED / WOOD

Blackberry, Cherry, Orange, Lemon, Nutty, Pepper, Ginger, Oak, Vanilla, Caramel, Tobacco, Leather, Spice, Butter, Wax, Bread, Bacon, Medicinal, Earth, Peaty

TASTE - OK, now take a sip. Roll it around. Describe it.

1. FIRST TASTE

Clean | Sweet | Sour | Salty | Bitter

2. FLAVOR

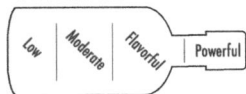

Low | Moderate | Flavorful | Powerful

3. PEATY

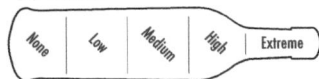

None | Low | Medium | High | Extreme

4. BODY

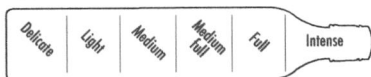

Delicate | Light | Medium | Medium Tall | Full | Intense

5. SWEETNESS

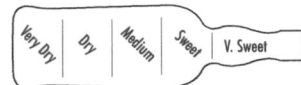

Very Dry | Dry | Medium | Sweet | V. Sweet

DOODLES & NOTES

6. FLAVOR GRAPH

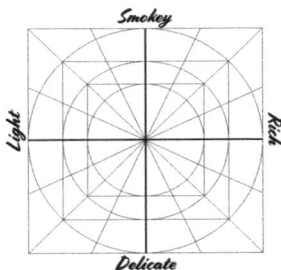

Smokey

Light

Rich

Delicate

MARK WITH A 🭩

7. FINISH

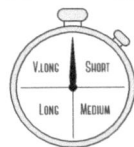

V.LONG | SHORT
LONG | MEDIUM

Describe it

8. BALANCE

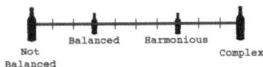

Not Balanced | Balanced | Harmonious | Complex

9. DEPTH

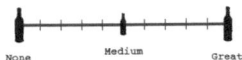

None | Medium | Great

10. OFF-FLAVORS?

OTHER THOUGHTS - What did you think of this one?

BOTTLE & LABEL

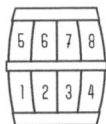

5 6 7 8
1 2 3 4

VALUE

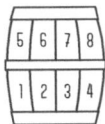

5 6 7 8
1 2 3 4

PRICE

DRINK AGAIN?

DESCRIBE IN 3 WORDS

_____

_____

_____

LOG:

Distillery _____ Region _____

Whiskey Name _____ Country _____

Type _____ ABV _____

Age _____ Unicorn? 👍 Rating 🥃🥃🥃🥃🥃

APPEARANCE - First, fill your glass! (Or draw your own)

| Swirling Glass | Vinum Single Malt | Large Glencairn | NEAT Glass | Wine | Glencairn | Straight Tumbler | Bourbon Tumbler | Draw Your Own! |

Now, hold it up against a white background. Describe what you see.

1. CLARITY

Watery, Pale — Medium — Opaque, Deep

2. VISCOSITY / LEGS

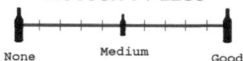

None — Medium — Good

3. COLOR & HUE

Lighter / Amber / Darker

Gin Clear	Pale Straw	Light Gold
Yellow Gold	Golden	Pale Amber
Rich Amber	Burnt Amber	Tawny
Mahogany	Old Oak	Treacle

4. DOODLES & NOTES

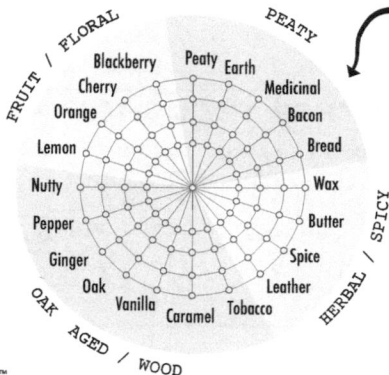

AROMA - Let's get your nose involved. Use the Aroma Wheel.

DOODLES & NOTES

Aroma Wheel labels:
FRUIT / FLORAL — PEATY — HERBAL / SPICY — OAK AGED / WOOD

Blackberry, Cherry, Orange, Lemon, Nutty, Pepper, Ginger, Oak, Vanilla, Caramel, Tobacco, Leather, Spice, Butter, Wax, Bread, Bacon, Medicinal, Earth, Peaty

THE WHISKEY TASTING DOODLE BOOK™

TASTE - OK, now take a sip. Roll it around. Describe it.

1. FIRST TASTE

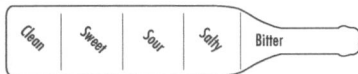

Clean | Sweet | Sour | Salty | Bitter

2. FLAVOR

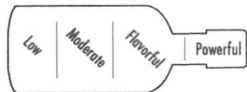

Low | Moderate | Flavorful | Powerful

3. PEATY

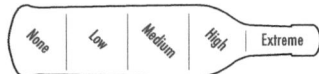

None | Low | Medium | High | Extreme

4. BODY

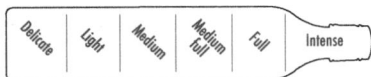

Delicate | Light | Medium | Medium full | Full | Intense

5. SWEETNESS

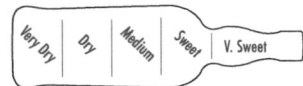

Very Dry | Dry | Medium | Sweet | V. Sweet

DOODLES & NOTES

6. FLAVOR GRAPH

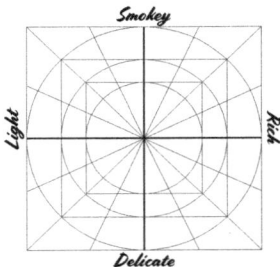

Smokey

Light

Rich

Delicate

MARK WITH A ●

7. FINISH

Describe it

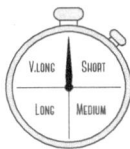

V.LONG | SHORT
LONG | MEDIUM

8. BALANCE

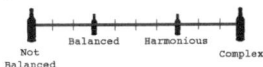

Not Balanced | Balanced | Harmonious | Complex

9. DEPTH

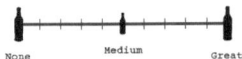

None | Medium | Great

10. OFF-FLAVORS?

OTHER THOUGHTS - What did you think of this one?

BOTTLE & LABEL

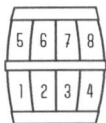

5 6 7 8
1 2 3 4

VALUE

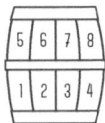

5 6 7 8
1 2 3 4

PRICE

DRINK AGAIN?

DESCRIBE IN 3 WORDS

_____
_____
_____

LOG:

Distillery _____ Region _____

Whiskey Name _____ Country _____

Type _____ ABV _____

Age _____ Unicorn? 👍 Rating 🥃🥃🥃🥃🥃

APPEARANCE - First, fill your glass! (Or draw your own)

| Swirling Glass | Vinum Single Malt | Large Glencairn | NEAT Glass | Wine | Glencairn | Straight Tumbler | Bourbon Tumbler | Draw Your Own! |

Now, hold it up against a white background. Describe what you see

1. CLARITY

Watery, Pale — Medium — Opaque, Deep

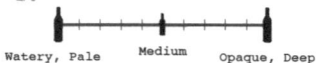

2. VISCOSITY / LEGS

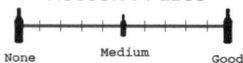

None — Medium — Good

3. COLOR & HUE

Lighter / Gold/Amber / Darker

Gin Clear	Pale Straw	Light Gold
Yellow Gold	Golden	Pale Amber
Rich Amber	Burnt Amber	Tawny
Mahogany	Old Oak	Treacle

4. DOODLES & NOTES

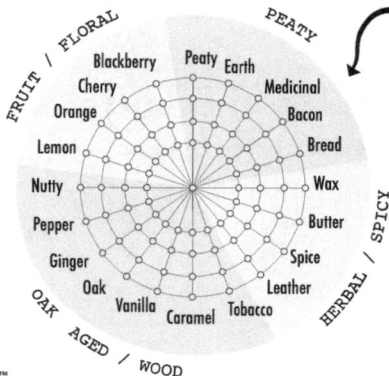

AROMA - Let's get your nose involved. Use the Aroma Wheel.

DOODLES & NOTES

FRUIT / FLORAL — PEATY — HERBAL / SPICY — OAK AGED / WOOD

Blackberry, Cherry, Orange, Lemon, Nutty, Pepper, Ginger, Oak, Vanilla, Caramel, Tobacco, Leather, Spice, Butter, Wax, Bread, Bacon, Medicinal, Earth, Peaty

THE WHISKEY TASTING DOODLE BOOK™

TASTE - OK, now take a sip. Roll it around. Describe it.

1. FIRST TASTE

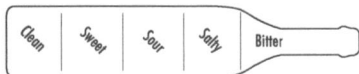

Clean | Sweet | Sour | Salty | Bitter

2. FLAVOR

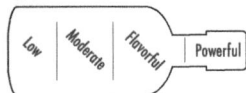

Low | Moderate | Flavorful | Powerful

3. PEATY

None | Low | Medium | High | Extreme

4. BODY

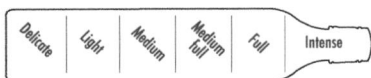

Delicate | Light | Medium | Medium Full | Full | Intense

5. SWEETNESS

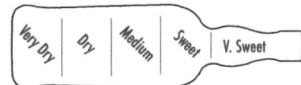

Very Dry | Dry | Medium | Sweet | V. Sweet

DOODLES & NOTES

6. FLAVOR GRAPH

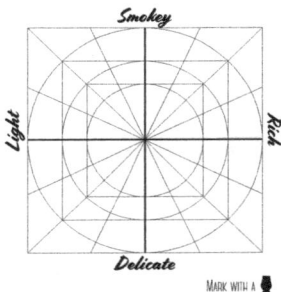

Smokey

Light

Rich

Delicate

MARK WITH A 🥃

7. FINISH

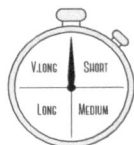

V.LONG | SHORT
LONG | MEDIUM

Describe it

8. BALANCE

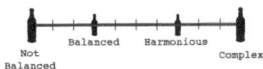

Not Balanced | Balanced | Harmonious | Complex

9. DEPTH

None | Medium | Great

10. OFF-FLAVORS?

OTHER THOUGHTS - What did you think of this one?

BOTTLE & LABEL

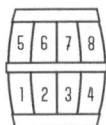

5 6 7 8
1 2 3 4

VALUE

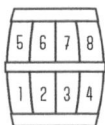

5 6 7 8
1 2 3 4

PRICE

DRINK AGAIN?

DESCRIBE IN 3 WORDS

LOG:

Distillery _____   Region _____

Whiskey Name _____   Country _____

Type _____   ABV _____

Age _____   Unicorn? 👍   Rating ⬙ ⬙ ⬙ ⬙ ⬙

APPEARANCE – First, fill your glass! (Or draw your own)

Swirling Glass   Vinum Single Malt   Large Glencairn   NEAT Glass   Wine   Glencairn   Straight Tumbler   Bourbon Tumbler   Draw Your Own!

Now, hold it up against a white background. Describe what you see

1. CLARITY

Watery, Pale   Medium   Opaque, Deep

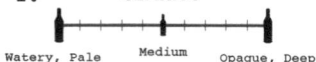

2. VISCOSITY / LEGS

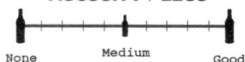

None   Medium   Good

3. COLOR & HUE

Lighter / Gold/Amber / Darker

Gin Clear	Pale Straw	Light Gold
Yellow Gold	Golden	Pale Amber
Rich Amber	Burnt Amber	Tawny
Mahogany	Old Oak	Treacle

4. DOODLES & NOTES

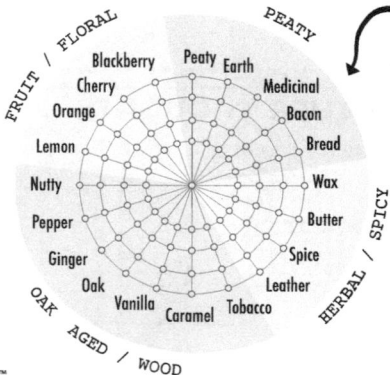

AROMA – Let's get your nose involved. Use the Aroma Wheel.

DOODLES & NOTES

FRUIT / FLORAL — PEATY

Blackberry, Cherry, Orange, Lemon, Nutty, Pepper, Ginger, Oak, Vanilla, Caramel, Tobacco, Leather, Spice, Butter, Wax, Bread, Bacon, Medicinal, Earth, Peaty

OAK AGED / WOOD — HERBAL / SPICY

THE WHISKEY TASTING DOODLE BOOK™

TASTE - OK, now take a sip. Roll it around. Describe it.

1. FIRST TASTE

Clean | Sweet | Sour | Salty | Bitter

2. FLAVOR
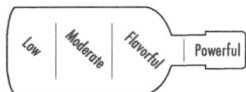
Low | Moderate | Flavorful | Powerful

3. PEATY
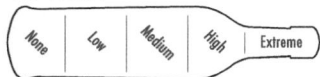
None | Low | Medium | High | Extreme

4. BODY

Delicate | Light | Medium | Medium full | Full | Intense

5. SWEETNESS
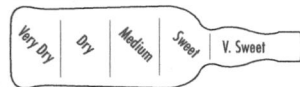
Very Dry | Dry | Medium | Sweet | V. Sweet

DOODLES & NOTES

6. FLAVOR GRAPH
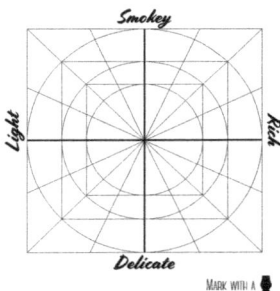
Smokey
Light
Rich
Delicate
MARK WITH A 🛢

7. FINISH

V. Long | Short | Long | Medium
Describe it

8. BALANCE
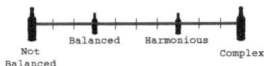
Not Balanced | Balanced | Harmonious | Complex

9. DEPTH
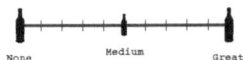
None | Medium | Great

10. OFF-FLAVORS?

OTHER THOUGHTS - What did you think of this one?

BOTTLE & LABEL
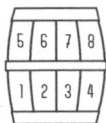
5 | 6 | 7 | 8
1 | 2 | 3 | 4

VALUE
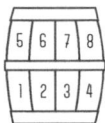
5 | 6 | 7 | 8
1 | 2 | 3 | 4

PRICE

DRINK AGAIN?

DESCRIBE IN 3 WORDS

LOG:

Distillery _____ Region _____

Whiskey Name _____ Country _____

Type _____ ABV _____

Age _____ Unicorn? 👍 Rating 🥃🥃🥃🥃🥃

APPEARANCE - First, fill your glass! (Or draw your own)

| Swirling Glass | Vinum Single Malt | Large Glencairn | NEAT Glass | Wine | Glencairn | Straight Tumbler | Bourbon Tumbler | Draw Your Own! |

Now, hold it up against a white background. Describe what you see

1.   CLARITY

Watery, Pale   Medium   Opaque, Deep

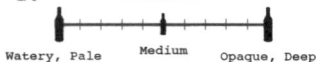

2.   VISCOSITY / LEGS

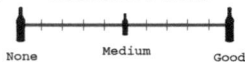

None   Medium   Good

3.   COLOR & HUE

Lighter
Gold/Amber
Darker

Gin Clear	Pale Straw	Light Gold
Yellow Gold	Golden	Pale Amber
Rich Amber	Burnt Amber	Tawny
Mahogany	Old Oak	Treacle

4.   DOODLES & NOTES

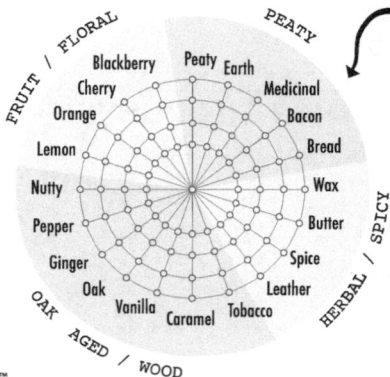

AROMA - Let's get your nose involved. Use the Aroma Wheel.

DOODLES & NOTES

Aroma Wheel:
FRUIT / FLORAL — PEATY — HERBAL / SPICY — OAK AGED / WOOD

Blackberry, Cherry, Orange, Lemon, Nutty, Pepper, Ginger, Oak, Vanilla, Caramel, Tobacco, Leather, Spice, Butter, Wax, Bread, Bacon, Medicinal, Earth, Peaty

TASTE - OK, now take a sip. Roll it around. Describe it.

1. FIRST TASTE

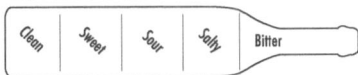

Clean | Sweet | Sour | Salty | Bitter

2. FLAVOR

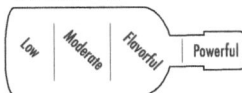

Low | Moderate | Flavorful | Powerful

3. PEATY

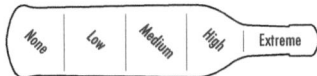

None | Low | Medium | High | Extreme

4. BODY

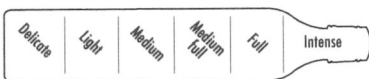

Delicate | Light | Medium | Medium Full | Full | Intense

5. SWEETNESS

Very Dry | Dry | Medium | Sweet | V. Sweet

DOODLES & NOTES

6. FLAVOR GRAPH

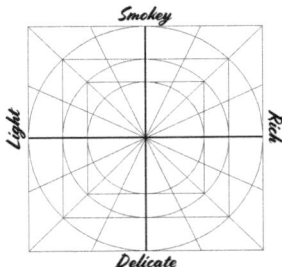

Smokey

Light

Rich

Delicate

MARK WITH A 🍶

7. FINISH

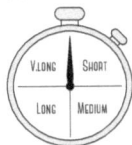

V.LONG | SHORT | LONG | MEDIUM

Describe it

8. BALANCE

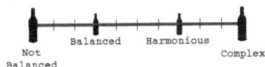

Not Balanced | Balanced | Harmonious | Complex

9. DEPTH

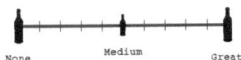

None | Medium | Great

10. OFF-FLAVORS?

OTHER THOUGHTS - What did you think of this one?

BOTTLE & LABEL

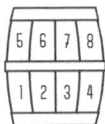

5 6 7 8
1 2 3 4

VALUE

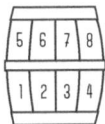

5 6 7 8
1 2 3 4

PRICE

DRINK AGAIN?

DESCRIBE IN 3 WORDS

Distillery _____   Region _____

Whiskey Name _____   Country _____

Type _____   ABV _____

Age _____   Unicorn? 👍   Rating 🥃🥃🥃🥃🥃

APPEARANCE - First, fill your glass! (Or draw your own)

Swirling Glass | Vinum Single Malt | Large Glencairn | NEAT Glass | Wine | Glencairn | Straight Tumbler | Bourbon Tumbler | Draw Your Own!

Now, hold it up against a white background. Describe what you see.

1. CLARITY

Watery, Pale — Medium — Opaque, Deep

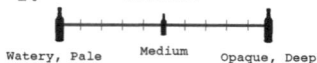

2. VISCOSITY / LEGS

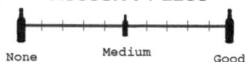

None — Medium — Good

3. COLOR & HUE

Lighter / Gold/Amber / Darker

Gin Clear	Pale Straw	Light Gold
Yellow Gold	Golden	Pale Amber
Rich Amber	Burnt Amber	Tawny
Mahogany	Old Oak	Treacle

4. DOODLES & NOTES

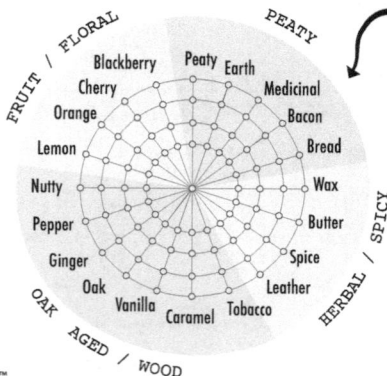

AROMA - Let's get your nose involved. Use the Aroma Wheel.

DOODLES & NOTES

Aroma Wheel categories: FRUIT / FLORAL, PEATY, HERBAL / SPICY, OAK / AGED / WOOD

Blackberry, Cherry, Orange, Lemon, Nutty, Pepper, Ginger, Oak, Vanilla, Caramel, Tobacco, Leather, Spice, Butter, Wax, Bread, Bacon, Medicinal, Earth, Peaty

TASTE - OK, now take a sip. Roll it around. Describe it.

1. FIRST TASTE
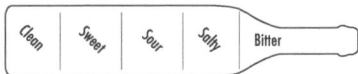
Clean | Sweet | Sour | Salty | Bitter

2. FLAVOR
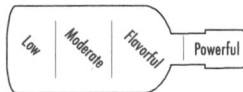
Low | Moderate | Flavorful | Powerful

3. PEATY

None | Low | Medium | High | Extreme

4. BODY
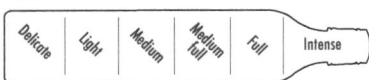
Delicate | Light | Medium | Medium full | Full | Intense

5. SWEETNESS
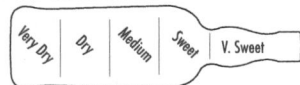
Very Dry | Dry | Medium | Sweet | V. Sweet

DOODLES & NOTES

6. FLAVOR GRAPH
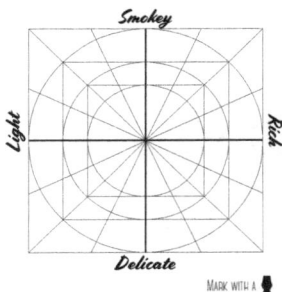
Smokey

Light

Rich

Delicate

MARK WITH A 🖤

7. FINISH
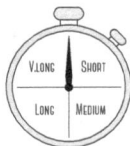
V.LONG | SHORT | LONG | MEDIUM

Describe it

8. BALANCE
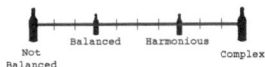
Not Balanced | Balanced | Harmonious | Complex

9. DEPTH
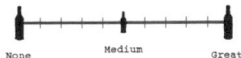
None | Medium | Great

10. OFF-FLAVORS?

OTHER THOUGHTS - What did you think of this one?

BOTTLE & LABEL
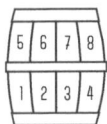
5 | 6 | 7 | 8
1 | 2 | 3 | 4

VALUE
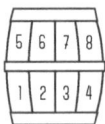
5 | 6 | 7 | 8
1 | 2 | 3 | 4

PRICE

DRINK AGAIN?

DESCRIBE IN 3 WORDS

LOG:

Distillery _____ Region _____

Whiskey Name _____ Country _____

Type _____ ABV _____

Age _____ Unicorn? 👍 Rating 🥃🥃🥃🥃🥃

APPEARANCE - First, fill your glass! (Or draw your own)

Swirling Glass | Vinum Single Malt | Large Glencairn | NEAT Glass | Wine | Glencairn | Straight Tumbler | Bourbon Tumbler | Draw Your Own!

Now, hold it up against a white background. Describe what you see

1. **CLARITY**

Watery, Pale — Medium — Opaque, Deep

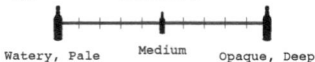

2. **VISCOSITY / LEGS**

None — Medium — Good

3. **COLOR & HUE**

Lighter
Gold/Amber
Darker

Gin Clear	Pale Straw	Light Gold
Yellow Gold	Golden	Pale Amber
Rich Amber	Burnt Amber	Tawny
Mahogany	Old Oak	Treacle

4. **DOODLES & NOTES**

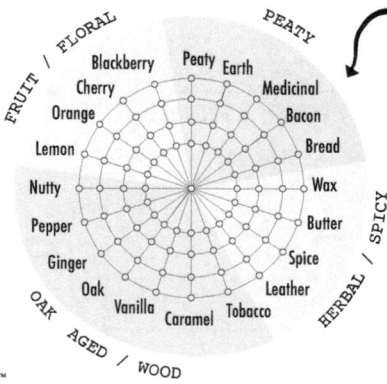

AROMA - Let's get your nose involved. Use the Aroma Wheel.

DOODLES & NOTES

Aroma Wheel — FLORAL / FRUIT / PEATY / HERBAL / SPICY / OAK AGED / WOOD: Blackberry, Peaty, Earth, Cherry, Medicinal, Orange, Bacon, Lemon, Bread, Nutty, Wax, Pepper, Butter, Ginger, Spice, Oak, Leather, Vanilla, Caramel, Tobacco

THE WHISKEY TASTING DOODLE BOOK™

TASTE - OK, now take a sip. Roll it around. Describe it.

1. FIRST TASTE

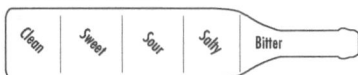

Clean | Sweet | Sour | Salty | Bitter

2. FLAVOR

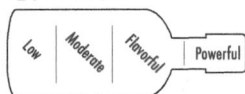

Low | Moderate | Flavorful | Powerful

3. PEATY

None | Low | Medium | High | Extreme

4. BODY

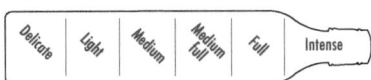

Delicate | Light | Medium | Medium full | Full | Intense

5. SWEETNESS

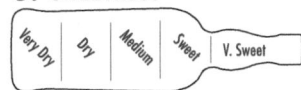

Very Dry | Dry | Medium | Sweet | V. Sweet

DOODLES & NOTES

6. FLAVOR GRAPH

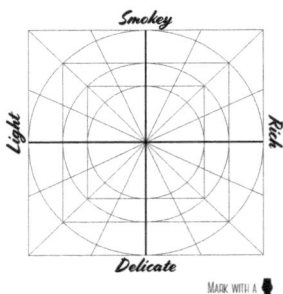

Smokey

Light

Rich

Delicate

MARK WITH A 🍸

7. FINISH

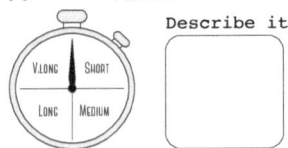

V. LONG | SHORT | LONG | MEDIUM

Describe it

8. BALANCE

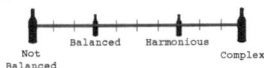

Not Balanced | Balanced | Harmonious | Complex

9. DEPTH

None | Medium | Great

10. OFF-FLAVORS?

OTHER THOUGHTS - What did you think of this one?

BOTTLE & LABEL

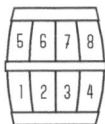

5 | 6 | 7 | 8
1 | 2 | 3 | 4

VALUE

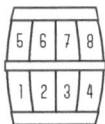

5 | 6 | 7 | 8
1 | 2 | 3 | 4

PRICE

DRINK AGAIN?

DESCRIBE IN 3 WORDS

_____

_____

_____

LOG:

Distillery _____   Region _____

Whiskey Name _____   Country _____

Type _____   ABV _____

Age _____   Unicorn? 👍   Rating ⟡ ⟡ ⟡ ⟡ ⟡

APPEARANCE - First, fill your glass! (Or draw your own)

Swirling Glass	Vinum Single Malt	Large Glencairn	NEAT Glass	Wine	Glencairn	Straight Tumbler	Bourbon Tumbler	Draw Your Own!

Now, hold it up against a white background. Describe what you see

1. CLARITY

Watery, Pale   Medium   Opaque, Deep

2. VISCOSITY / LEGS

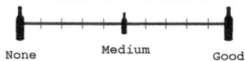

None   Medium   Good

3. COLOR & HUE

Lighter	Gin Clear	Pale Straw	Light Gold
Gold/Amber	Yellow Gold	Golden	Pale Amber
	Rich Amber	Burnt Amber	Tawny
Darker	Mahogany	Old Oak	Treacle

4. DOODLES & NOTES

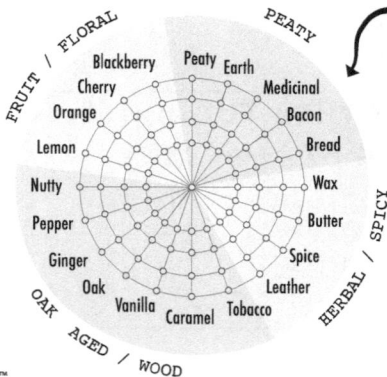

AROMA - Let's get your nose involved. Use the Aroma Wheel.

DOODLES & NOTES

FRUIT / FLORAL — PEATY
Blackberry, Cherry, Orange, Lemon, Nutty, Pepper, Ginger, Oak, Vanilla, Caramel, Tobacco, Leather, Spice, Butter, Wax, Bread, Bacon, Medicinal, Peaty Earth

OAK AGED / WOOD — HERBAL / SPICY

THE WHISKEY TASTING DOODLE BOOK™

TASTE - OK, now take a sip. Roll it around. Describe it.

1. FIRST TASTE

Clean | Sweet | Sour | Salty | Bitter

2. FLAVOR

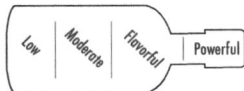

Low | Moderate | Flavorful | Powerful

3. PEATY

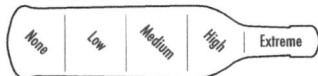

None | Low | Medium | High | Extreme

4. BODY

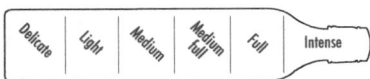

Delicate | Light | Medium | Medium Full | Full | Intense

5. SWEETNESS

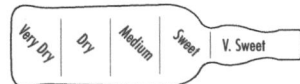

Very Dry | Dry | Medium | Sweet | V. Sweet

DOODLES & NOTES

6. FLAVOR GRAPH

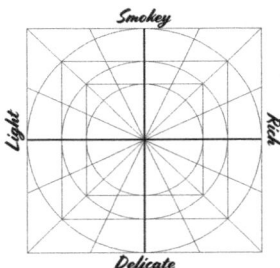

Smokey

Light | Rich

Delicate

Mark with a ●

7. FINISH

V.LONG | SHORT | LONG | MEDIUM

Describe it

8. BALANCE

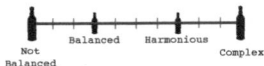

Not Balanced | Balanced | Harmonious | Complex

9. DEPTH

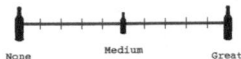

None | Medium | Great

10. OFF-FLAVORS?

OTHER THOUGHTS - What did you think of this one?

BOTTLE & LABEL

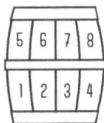

5 6 7 8
1 2 3 4

VALUE

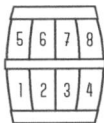

5 6 7 8
1 2 3 4

PRICE

DRINK AGAIN?

DESCRIBE IN 3 WORDS

THE WHISKEY TASTING DOODLE BOOK™

LOG:

Distillery _____ Region _____

Whiskey Name _____ Country _____

Type _____ ABV _____

Age _____ Unicorn? 👍 Rating 🥃🥃🥃🥃🥃

APPEARANCE – First, fill your glass! (Or draw your own)

Swirling Glass | Vinum Single Malt | Large Glencairn | NEAT Glass | Wine | Glencairn | Straight Tumbler | Bourbon Tumbler | Draw Your Own!

Now, hold it up against a white background. Describe what you see.

1. CLARITY

Watery, Pale — Medium — Opaque, Deep

2. VISCOSITY / LEGS

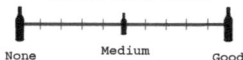

None — Medium — Good

3. COLOR & HUE

Lighter / Gold/Amber / Darker

Gin Clear	Pale Straw	Light Gold
Yellow Gold	Golden	Pale Amber
Rich Amber	Burnt Amber	Tawny
Mahogany	Old Oak	Treacle

4. DOODLES & NOTES

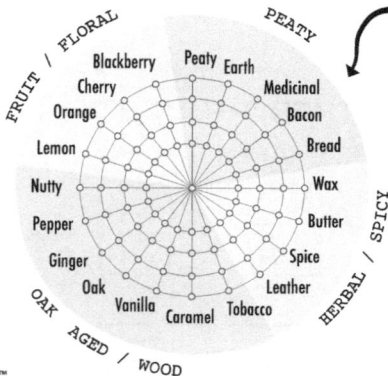

AROMA – Let's get your nose involved. Use the Aroma Wheel.

DOODLES & NOTES

FRUIT / FLORAL — PEATY — SPICY — HERBAL / SPICY — OAK AGED / WOOD

Blackberry, Cherry, Orange, Lemon, Nutty, Pepper, Ginger, Oak, Vanilla, Caramel, Tobacco, Leather, Spice, Butter, Wax, Bread, Bacon, Medicinal, Earth, Peaty

THE WHISKEY TASTING DOODLE BOOK™

TASTE - OK, now take a sip. Roll it around. Describe it.

1. FIRST TASTE

Clean | Sweet | Sour | Salty | Bitter

2. FLAVOR

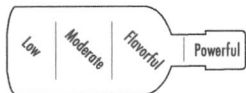

Low | Moderate | Flavorful | Powerful

3. PEATY

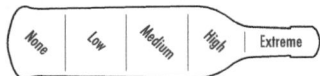

None | Low | Medium | High | Extreme

4. BODY

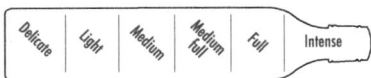

Delicate | Light | Medium | Medium full | Full | Intense

5. SWEETNESS

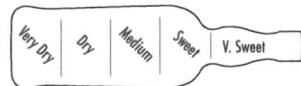

Very Dry | Dry | Medium | Sweet | V. Sweet

DOODLES & NOTES

6. FLAVOR GRAPH

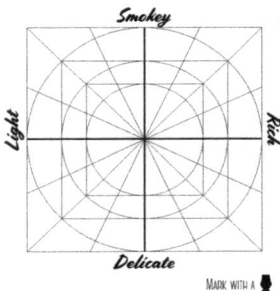

Smokey / Light / Rich / Delicate

MARK WITH A ⬛

7. FINISH

V. Long | Short | Long | Medium

Describe it

8. BALANCE

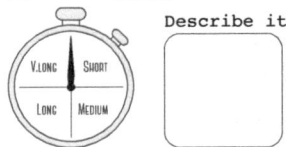

Not Balanced | Balanced | Harmonious | Complex

9. DEPTH

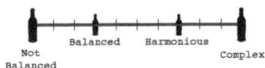

None | Medium | Great

10. OFF-FLAVORS?

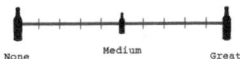

OTHER THOUGHTS - What did you think of this one?

BOTTLE & LABEL

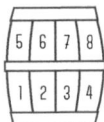

5 6 7 8
1 2 3 4

VALUE

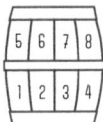

5 6 7 8
1 2 3 4

PRICE

DRINK AGAIN?

DESCRIBE IN 3 WORDS

_____
_____
_____

Distillery _____   Region _____

Whiskey Name _____   Country _____

Type _____   ABV _____

Age _____   Unicorn? 👍   Rating 🥃 🥃 🥃 🥃 🥃

APPEARANCE -First, fill your glass! (Or draw your own)

| Swirling Glass | Vinum Single Malt | Large Glencairn | NEAT Glass | Wine | Glencairn | Straight Tumbler | Bourbon Tumbler | Draw Your Own! |

Now, hold it up against a white background. Describe what you see.

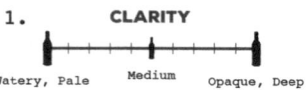

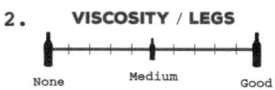

1.   CLARITY

Watery, Pale   Medium   Opaque, Deep

2.   VISCOSITY / LEGS

None   Medium   Good

3.   COLOR & HUE

Lighter
ld/Amber
Darker

Gin Clear	Pale Straw	Light Gold
Yellow Gold	Golden	Pale Amber
Rich Amber	Burnt Amber	Tawny
Mahogany	Old Oak	Treacle

4.   DOODLES & NOTES

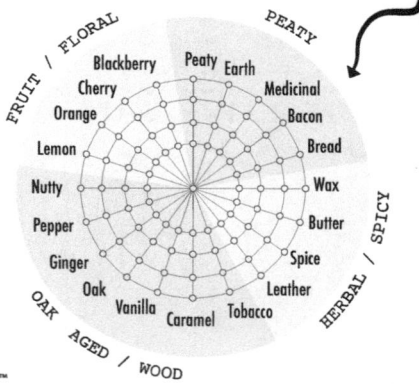

AROMA - Let's get your nose involved. Use the Aroma Wheel.

DOODLES & NOTES

Aroma Wheel labels:
FRUIT / FLORAL — Blackberry, Cherry, Orange, Lemon, Nutty, Pepper
PEATY — Peaty, Earth, Medicinal, Bacon, Bread, Wax, Butter
HERBAL / SPICY — Spice, Leather, Tobacco
OAK AGED / WOOD — Ginger, Oak, Vanilla, Caramel

THE WHISKEY TASTING DOODLE BOOK™

TASTE - OK, now take a sip. Roll it around. Describe it.

1. FIRST TASTE

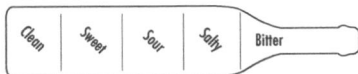
Clean | Sweet | Sour | Salty | Bitter

2. FLAVOR

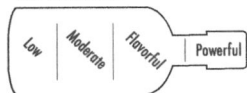
Low | Moderate | Flavorful | Powerful

3. PEATY

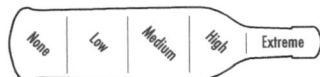
None | Low | Medium | High | Extreme

4. BODY

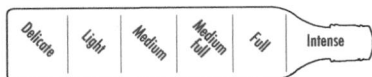
Delicate | Light | Medium | Medium Full | Full | Intense

5. SWEETNESS

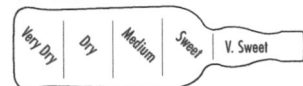
Very Dry | Dry | Medium | Sweet | V. Sweet

DOODLES & NOTES

6. FLAVOR GRAPH

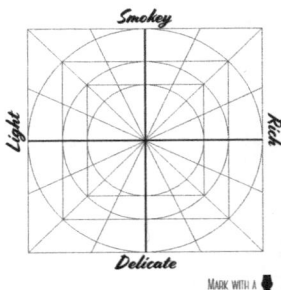
Smokey | Light | Rich | Delicate

MARK WITH A

7. FINISH

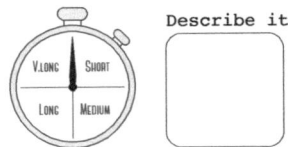
V. LONG | SHORT | LONG | MEDIUM

Describe it

8. BALANCE

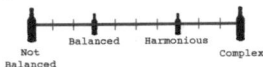
Not Balanced | Balanced | Harmonious | Complex

9. DEPTH

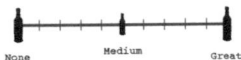
None | Medium | Great

10. OFF-FLAVORS?

OTHER THOUGHTS - What did you think of this one?

BOTTLE & LABEL

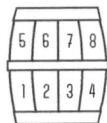
5 6 7 8
1 2 3 4

VALUE

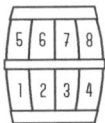
5 6 7 8
1 2 3 4

PRICE

DRINK AGAIN?

DESCRIBE IN 3 WORDS

LOG:

Distillery _____ Region _____

Whiskey Name _____ Country _____

Type _____ ABV _____

Age _____ Unicorn? 👍 Rating 🥃🥃🥃🥃🥃

APPEARANCE – First, fill your glass! (Or draw your own)

Swirling Glass | Vinum Single Malt | Large Glencairn | NEAT Glass | Wine | Glencairn | Straight Tumbler | Bourbon Tumbler | Draw Your Own!

Now, hold it up against a white background. Describe what you see.

1. CLARITY

Watery, Pale   Medium   Opaque, Deep

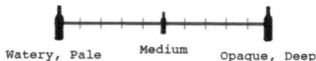

2. VISCOSITY / LEGS

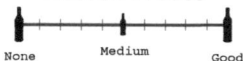

None   Medium   Good

3. COLOR & HUE

Lighter / Amber / Darker

Gin Clear	Pale Straw	Light Gold
Yellow Gold	Golden	Pale Amber
Rich Amber	Burnt Amber	Tawny
Mahogany	Old Oak	Treacle

4. DOODLES & NOTES

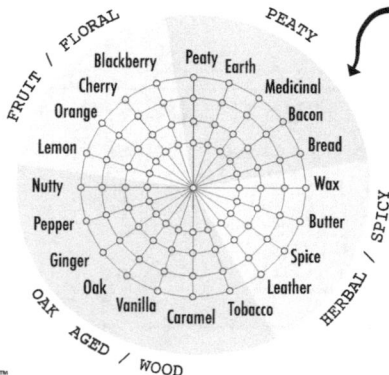

AROMA – Let's get your nose involved. Use the Aroma Wheel.

DOODLES & NOTES

FRUIT / FLORAL
Blackberry, Cherry, Orange, Lemon, Nutty, Pepper, Ginger, Oak, Vanilla, Caramel, Tobacco, Leather, Spice, Butter, Wax, Bread, Bacon, Medicinal, Earth, Peaty

PEATY

HERBAL / SPICY

OAK AGED / WOOD

TASTE - OK, now take a sip. Roll it around. Describe it.

1. FIRST TASTE

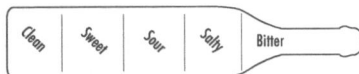

Clean | Sweet | Sour | Salty | Bitter

2. FLAVOR

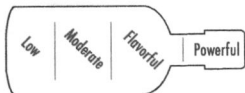

Low | Moderate | Flavorful | Powerful

3. PEATY

None | Low | Medium | High | Extreme

4. BODY

Delicate | Light | Medium | Medium full | Full | Intense

5. SWEETNESS

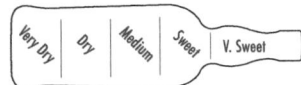

Very Dry | Dry | Medium | Sweet | V. Sweet

DOODLES & NOTES

6. FLAVOR GRAPH

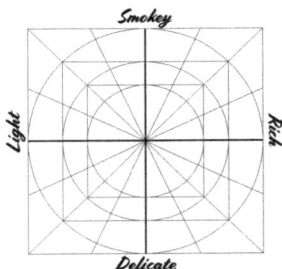

Smokey · Light · Rich · Delicate

MARK WITH A ●

7. FINISH

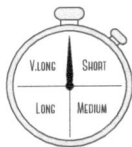

V. LONG | SHORT | LONG | MEDIUM

Describe it

8. BALANCE

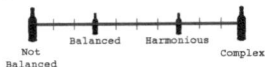

Not Balanced | Balanced | Harmonious | Complex

9. DEPTH

None | Medium | Great

10. OFF-FLAVORS?

OTHER THOUGHTS - What did you think of this one?

BOTTLE & LABEL

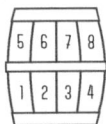

5 | 6 | 7 | 8
1 | 2 | 3 | 4

VALUE

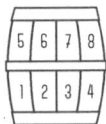

5 | 6 | 7 | 8
1 | 2 | 3 | 4

PRICE

DRINK AGAIN?

DESCRIBE IN 3 WORDS

_____
_____
_____

LOG:

Distillery _____ Region _____

Whiskey Name _____ Country _____

Type _____ ABV _____

Age _____ Unicorn? 👍 Rating 🥃🥃🥃🥃🥃

APPEARANCE – First, fill your glass! (Or draw your own)

Swirling Glass	Vinum Single Malt	Large Glencairn	NEAT Glass	Wine	Glencairn	Straight Tumbler	Bourbon Tumbler	Draw Your Own!

Now, hold it up against a white background. Describe what you see

1. **CLARITY**

Watery, Pale — Medium — Opaque, Deep

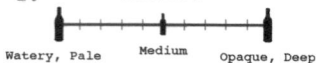

2. **VISCOSITY / LEGS**

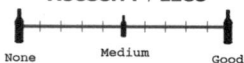

None — Medium — Good

3. **COLOR & HUE**

Lighter
Gold/Amber
Darker

Gin Clear	Pale Straw	Light Gold
Yellow Gold	Golden	Pale Amber
Rich Amber	Burnt Amber	Tawny
Mahogany	Old Oak	Treacle

4. **DOODLES & NOTES**

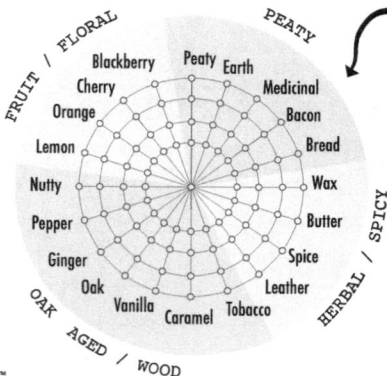

AROMA – Let's get your nose involved. Use the Aroma Wheel.▸

DOODLES & NOTES

FRUIT / FLORAL — PEATY

Blackberry, Cherry, Orange, Lemon, Nutty, Pepper, Ginger, Oak, Vanilla, Caramel, Tobacco, Leather, Spice, Butter, Wax, Bread, Bacon, Medicinal, Earth, Peaty

HERBAL / SPICY

OAK / AGED / WOOD

THE WHISKEY TASTING DOODLE BOOK™

TASTE - OK, now take a sip. Roll it around. Describe it.

1. FIRST TASTE

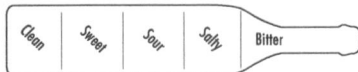
Clean | Sweet | Sour | Salty | Bitter

2. FLAVOR

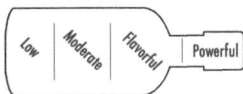
Low | Moderate | Flavorful | Powerful

3. PEATY

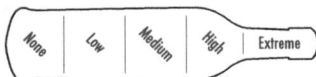
None | Low | Medium | High | Extreme

4. BODY

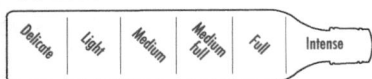
Delicate | Light | Medium | Medium full | Full | Intense

5. SWEETNESS

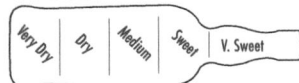
Very Dry | Dry | Medium | Sweet | V. Sweet

DOODLES & NOTES

6. FLAVOR GRAPH

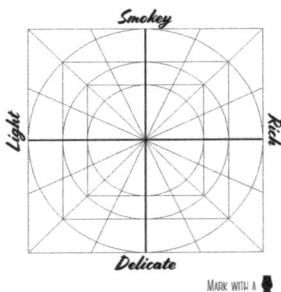
Smokey
Light
Rich
Delicate

MARK WITH A

7. FINISH

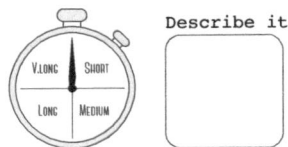
V.LONG | SHORT
LONG | MEDIUM

Describe it

8. BALANCE

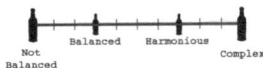
Not Balanced | Balanced | Harmonious | Complex

9. DEPTH

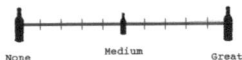
None | Medium | Great

10. OFF-FLAVORS?

OTHER THOUGHTS - What did you think of this one?

BOTTLE & LABEL

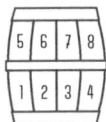
5 6 7 8
1 2 3 4

VALUE

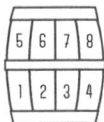
5 6 7 8
1 2 3 4

PRICE

DRINK AGAIN?

DESCRIBE IN 3 WORDS

THE WHISKEY TASTING DOODLE BOOK™

LOG:

Distillery _____   Region _____

Whiskey Name _____   Country _____

Type _____   ABV _____

Age _____   Unicorn? 👍   Rating ⟨ ⟩ ⟨ ⟩ ⟨ ⟩ ⟨ ⟩ ⟨ ⟩

APPEARANCE - First, fill your glass! (Or draw your own)

| Swirling Glass | Vinum Single Malt | Large Glencairn | NEAT Glass | Wine | Glencairn | Straight Tumbler | Bourbon Tumbler | Draw Your Own! |

Now, hold it up against a white background. Describe what you see

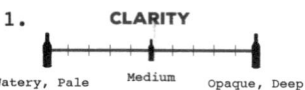

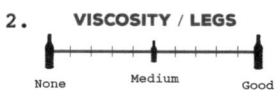

1.   CLARITY

Watery, Pale — Medium — Opaque, Deep

2.   VISCOSITY / LEGS

None — Medium — Good

3.   COLOR & HUE

Lighter
Gold/Amber
Darker

Gin Clear	Pale Straw	Light Gold
Yellow Gold	Golden	Pale Amber
Rich Amber	Burnt Amber	Tawny
Mahogany	Old Oak	Treacle

4.   DOODLES & NOTES

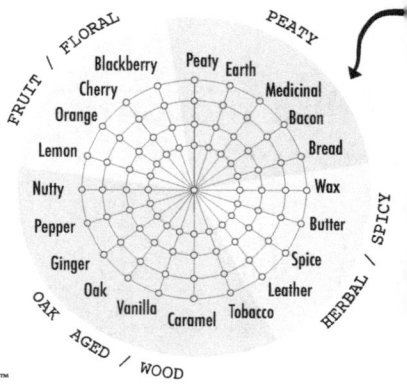

AROMA - Let's get your nose involved. Use the Aroma Wheel.

DOODLES & NOTES

FRUIT / FLORAL
PEATY
HERBAL / SPICY
OAK AGED / WOOD

Blackberry   Peaty   Earth
Cherry   Medicinal
Orange   Bacon
Lemon   Bread
Nutty   Wax
Pepper   Butter
Ginger   Spice
Oak   Leather
Vanilla   Caramel   Tobacco

THE WHISKEY TASTING DOODLE BOOK™

TASTE - OK, now take a sip. Roll it around. Describe it.

1. FIRST TASTE

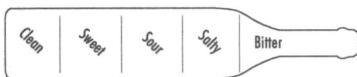

Clean | Sweet | Sour | Salty | Bitter

2. FLAVOR

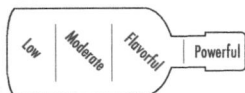

Low | Moderate | Flavorful | Powerful

3. PEATY

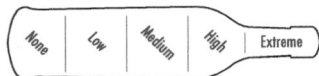

None | Low | Medium | High | Extreme

4. BODY

Delicate | Light | Medium | Medium full | Full | Intense

5. SWEETNESS

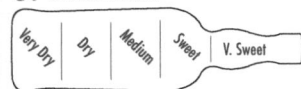

Very Dry | Dry | Medium | Sweet | V. Sweet

DOODLES & NOTES

6. FLAVOR GRAPH

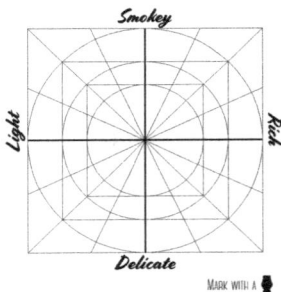

Smokey

Light

Rich

Delicate

MARK WITH A 🖤

7. FINISH

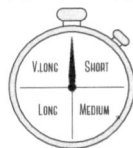

V. LONG | SHORT
LONG | MEDIUM

Describe it

8. BALANCE

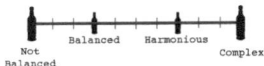

Not Balanced | Balanced | Harmonious | Complex

9. DEPTH

None | Medium | Great

10. OFF-FLAVORS?

OTHER THOUGHTS - What did you think of this one?

BOTTLE & LABEL

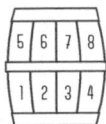

5 | 6 | 7 | 8
1 | 2 | 3 | 4

VALUE

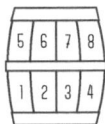

5 | 6 | 7 | 8
1 | 2 | 3 | 4

PRICE

DRINK AGAIN?

DESCRIBE IN 3 WORDS

_____
_____
_____

Distillery _____   Region _____

Whiskey Name _____   Country _____

Type _____   ABV _____

Age _____   Unicorn? 👍   Rating ⚖ ⚖ ⚖ ⚖ ⚖

APPEARANCE - First, fill your glass! (Or draw your own)

| Swirling Glass | Vinum Single Malt | Large Glencairn | NEAT Glass | Wine | Glencairn | Straight Tumbler | Bourbon Tumbler | Draw Your Own! |

Now, hold it up against a white background. Describe what you see

1. CLARITY

Watery, Pale — Medium — Opaque, Deep

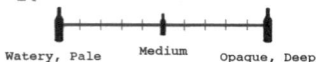

2. VISCOSITY / LEGS

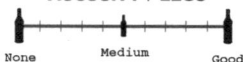

None — Medium — Good

3. COLOR & HUE

Lighter / Gold/Amber / Darker

Gin Clear	Pale Straw	Light Gold
Yellow Gold	Golden	Pale Amber
Rich Amber	Burnt Amber	Tawny
Mahogany	Old Oak	Treacle

4. DOODLES & NOTES

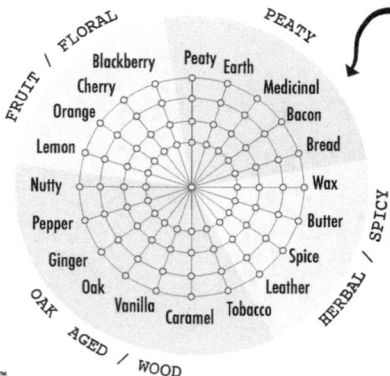

AROMA - Let's get your nose involved. Use the Aroma Wheel.

DOODLES & NOTES

FRUIT / FLORAL — PEATY — HERBAL / SPICY — OAK AGED / WOOD

Blackberry, Cherry, Orange, Lemon, Nutty, Pepper, Ginger, Oak, Vanilla, Caramel, Tobacco, Leather, Spice, Butter, Wax, Bread, Bacon, Medicinal, Earth, Peaty

THE WHISKEY TASTING DOODLE BOOK™

TASTE - OK, now take a sip. Roll it around. Describe it.

1. FIRST TASTE

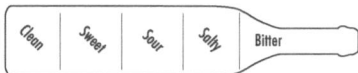

Clean | Sweet | Sour | Salty | Bitter

2. FLAVOR

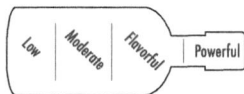

Low | Moderate | Flavorful | Powerful

3. PEATY

None | Low | Medium | High | Extreme

4. BODY

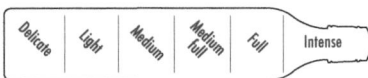

Delicate | Light | Medium | Medium Full | Full | Intense

5. SWEETNESS

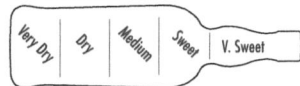

Very Dry | Dry | Medium | Sweet | V. Sweet

DOODLES & NOTES

6. FLAVOR GRAPH

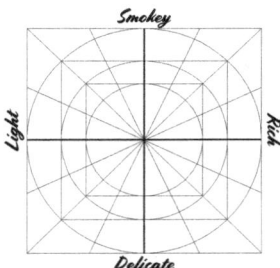

Smokey

Light

Rich

Delicate

MARK WITH A

7. FINISH

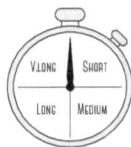

V.Long | Short | Long | Medium

Describe it

8. BALANCE

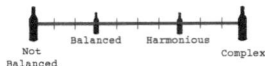

Not Balanced | Balanced | Harmonious | Complex

9. DEPTH

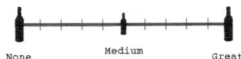

None | Medium | Great

10. OFF-FLAVORS?

OTHER THOUGHTS - What did you think of this one?

BOTTLE & LABEL

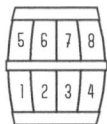

5 | 6 | 7 | 8
1 | 2 | 3 | 4

VALUE

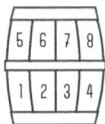

5 | 6 | 7 | 8
1 | 2 | 3 | 4

PRICE

DRINK AGAIN?

DESCRIBE IN 3 WORDS

LOG:

Distillery _____   Region _____

Whiskey Name _____   Country _____

Type _____   ABV _____

Age _____   Unicorn? 👍   Rating 🥃🥃🥃🥃🥃

APPEARANCE - First, fill your glass! (Or draw your own)

| Swirling Glass | Vinum Single Malt | Large Glencairn | NEAT Glass | Wine | Glencairn | Straight Tumbler | Bourbon Tumbler | Draw Your Own! |

Now, hold it up against a white background. Describe what you see.

1.   CLARITY

Watery, Pale   Medium   Opaque, Deep

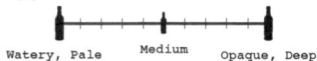

2.   VISCOSITY / LEGS

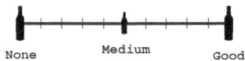

None   Medium   Good

3.   COLOR & HUE

Lighter
old/Amber
Darker

Gin Clear	Pale Straw	Light Gold
Yellow Gold	Golden	Pale Amber
Rich Amber	Burnt Amber	Tawny
Mahogany	Old Oak	Treacle

4.   DOODLES & NOTES

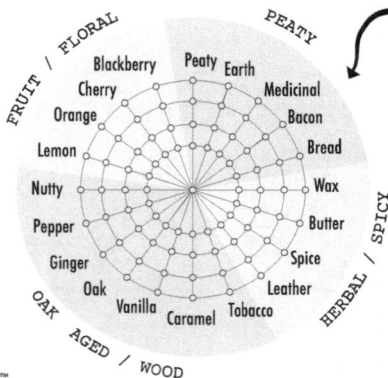

AROMA - Let's get your nose involved. Use the Aroma Wheel.➤

DOODLES & NOTES

FRUIT / FLORAL · PEATY · HERBAL / SPICY · OAK AGED / WOOD

Blackberry, Cherry, Orange, Lemon, Nutty, Pepper, Ginger, Oak, Vanilla, Caramel, Tobacco, Leather, Spice, Butter, Wax, Bread, Bacon, Medicinal, Earth, Peaty

THE WHISKEY TASTING DOODLE BOOK™

TASTE - OK, now take a sip. Roll it around. Describe it.

1. FIRST TASTE

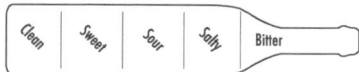

Clean | Sweet | Sour | Salty | Bitter

2. FLAVOR

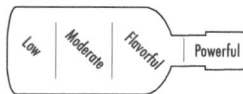

Low | Moderate | Flavorful | Powerful

3. PEATY

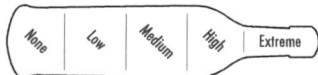

None | Low | Medium | High | Extreme

4. BODY

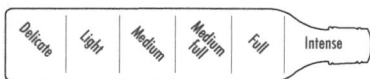

Delicate | Light | Medium | Medium full | Full | Intense

5. SWEETNESS

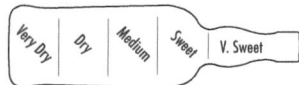

Very Dry | Dry | Medium | Sweet | V. Sweet

DOODLES & NOTES

6. FLAVOR GRAPH

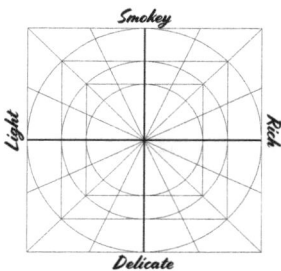

Smokey

Light

Rich

Delicate

MARK WITH A ⬇

7. FINISH

V.LONG | SHORT
LONG | MEDIUM

Describe it

8. BALANCE

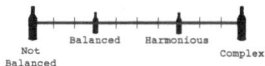

Not Balanced | Balanced | Harmonious | Complex

9. DEPTH

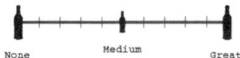

None | Medium | Great

10. OFF-FLAVORS?

OTHER THOUGHTS - What did you think of this one?

BOTTLE & LABEL

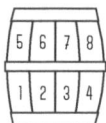

5 6 7 8
1 2 3 4

VALUE

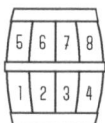

5 6 7 8
1 2 3 4

PRICE

DRINK AGAIN?

DESCRIBE IN 3 WORDS

_____
_____
_____

Distillery _____	Region _____
Whiskey Name _____	Country _____
Type _____	ABV _____
Age _____ Unicorn? 👍	Rating 🥃🥃🥃🥃🥃

APPEARANCE — First, fill your glass! (Or draw your own)

Swirling Glass | Vinum Single Malt | Large Glencairn | NEAT Glass | Wine | Glencairn | Straight Tumbler | Bourbon Tumbler | Draw Your Own!

Now, hold it up against a white background. Describe what you see

1. CLARITY

Watery, Pale — Medium — Opaque, Deep

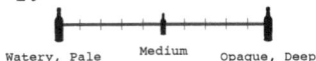

2. VISCOSITY / LEGS

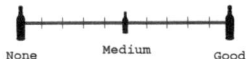

None — Medium — Good

3. COLOR & HUE

Lighter / Gold/Amber / Darker

Gin Clear	Pale Straw	Light Gold
Yellow Gold	Golden	Pale Amber
Rich Amber	Burnt Amber	Tawny
Mahogany	Old Oak	Treacle

4. DOODLES & NOTES

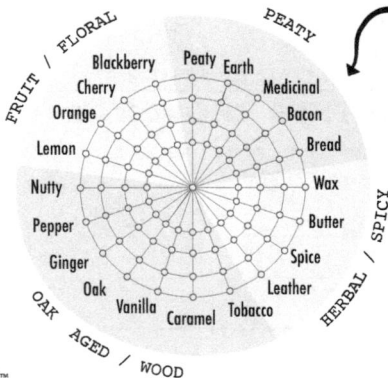

AROMA — Let's get your nose involved. Use the Aroma Wheel.

DOODLES & NOTES

Aroma Wheel labels: FRUIT / FLORAL, PEATY, Blackberry, Peaty, Earth, Cherry, Medicinal, Orange, Bacon, Lemon, Bread, Nutty, Wax, Pepper, Butter, Ginger, Spice, Oak, Leather, Vanilla, Caramel, Tobacco, HERBAL / SPICY, OAK AGED / WOOD

THE WHISKEY TASTING DOODLE BOOK™

TASTE - OK, now take a sip. Roll it around. Describe it.

1. FIRST TASTE

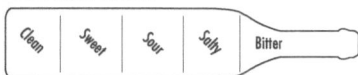

Clean | Sweet | Sour | Salty | Bitter

2. FLAVOR

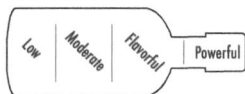

Low | Moderate | Flavorful | Powerful

3. PEATY

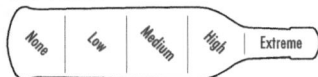

None | Low | Medium | High | Extreme

4. BODY

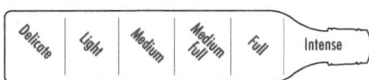

Delicate | Light | Medium | Medium Full | Full | Intense

5. SWEETNESS

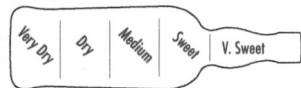

Very Dry | Dry | Medium | Sweet | V. Sweet

DOODLES & NOTES

6. FLAVOR GRAPH

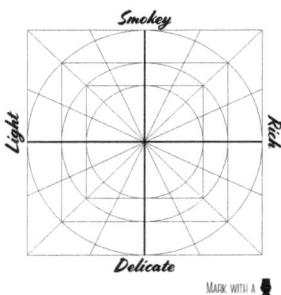

Smokey

Light

Rich

Delicate

Mark with a 🍾

7. FINISH

V. Long | Short
Long | Medium

Describe it

8. BALANCE

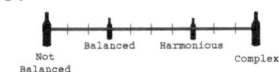

Not Balanced | Balanced | Harmonious | Complex

9. DEPTH

None | Medium | Great

10. OFF-FLAVORS?

OTHER THOUGHTS - What did you think of this one?

BOTTLE & LABEL

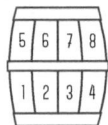

5 | 6 | 7 | 8
1 | 2 | 3 | 4

VALUE

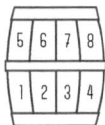

5 | 6 | 7 | 8
1 | 2 | 3 | 4

PRICE

DRINK AGAIN?

DESCRIBE IN 3 WORDS

_____
_____
_____

LOG:

Distillery _____	Region _____
Whiskey Name _____	Country _____
Type _____	ABV _____
Age _____ Unicorn? 👍	Rating 🥃🥃🥃🥃🥃

APPEARANCE - First, fill your glass! (Or draw your own)

Swirling Glass | Vinum Single Malt | Large Glencairn | NEAT Glass | Wine | Glencairn | Straight Tumbler | Bourbon Tumbler | Draw Your Own!

Now, hold it up against a white background. Describe what you see

1. CLARITY

Watery, Pale — Medium — Opaque, Deep

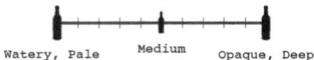

2. VISCOSITY / LEGS

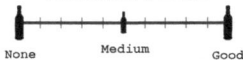

None — Medium — Good

3. COLOR & HUE

Lighter / Gold/Amber / Darker

Gin Clear	Pale Straw	Light Gold
Yellow Gold	Golden	Pale Amber
Rich Amber	Burnt Amber	Tawny
Mahogany	Old Oak	Treacle

4. DOODLES & NOTES

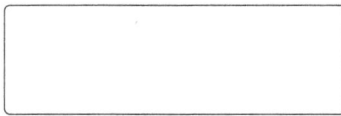

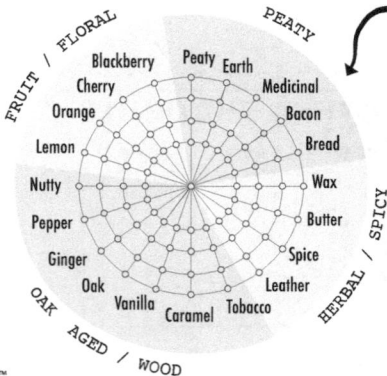

AROMA - Let's get your nose involved. Use the Aroma Wheel.

DOODLES & NOTES

FRUIT / FLORAL — PEATY — HERBAL / SPICY — OAK / AGED / WOOD

Blackberry, Cherry, Orange, Lemon, Nutty, Pepper, Ginger, Oak, Vanilla, Caramel, Tobacco, Leather, Spice, Butter, Wax, Bread, Bacon, Medicinal, Earth, Peaty

THE WHISKEY TASTING DOODLE BOOK™

TASTE - OK, now take a sip. Roll it around. Describe it.

1. FIRST TASTE

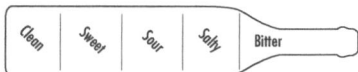

Clean | Sweet | Sour | Salty | Bitter

2. FLAVOR

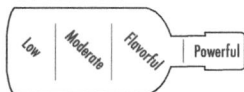

Low | Moderate | Flavorful | Powerful

3. PEATY

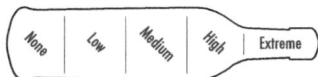

None | Low | Medium | High | Extreme

4. BODY

Delicate | Light | Medium | Medium full | Full | Intense

5. SWEETNESS

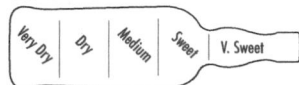

Very Dry | Dry | Medium | Sweet | V. Sweet

DOODLES & NOTES

6. FLAVOR GRAPH

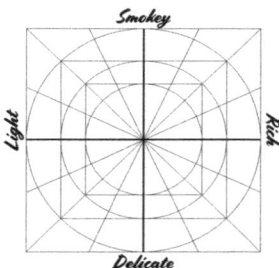

Smokey

Light

Rich

Delicate

MARK WITH A 🌶

7. FINISH

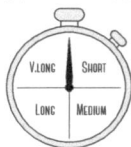

V. LONG | SHORT
LONG | MEDIUM

Describe it

8. BALANCE

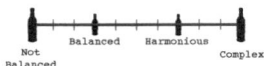

Not Balanced | Balanced | Harmonious | Complex

9. DEPTH

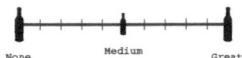

None | Medium | Great

10. OFF-FLAVORS?

OTHER THOUGHTS - What did you think of this one?

BOTTLE & LABEL

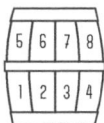

5 | 6 | 7 | 8
1 | 2 | 3 | 4

VALUE

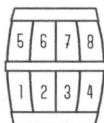

5 | 6 | 7 | 8
1 | 2 | 3 | 4

PRICE

DRINK AGAIN?

DESCRIBE IN 3 WORDS

THE WHISKEY TASTING DOODLE BOOK™

LOG:

Distillery _____   Region _____

Whiskey Name _____   Country _____

Type _____   ABV _____

Age _____   Unicorn? 👍   Rating ⛀ ⛀ ⛀ ⛀ ⛀

APPEARANCE – First, fill your glass! (Or draw your own)

Swirling Glass | Vinum Single Malt | Large Glencairn | NEAT Glass | Wine | Glencairn | Straight Tumbler | Bourbon Tumbler | Draw Your Own!

Now, hold it up against a white background. Describe what you see.

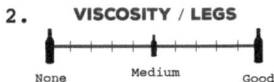

1.   CLARITY

Watery, Pale — Medium — Opaque, Deep

2.   VISCOSITY / LEGS

None — Medium — Good

3.   COLOR & HUE

Lighter
ld/Amber
Darker

Gin Clear	Pale Straw	Light Gold
Yellow Gold	Golden	Pale Amber
Rich Amber	Burnt Amber	Tawny
Mahogany	Old Oak	Treacle

4.   DOODLES & NOTES

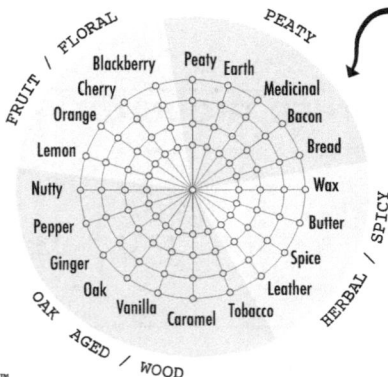

AROMA – Let's get your nose involved. Use the Aroma Wheel.

DOODLES & NOTES

FRUIT / FLORAL
PEATY
OAK AGED / WOOD
HERBAL / SPICY

Blackberry, Cherry, Orange, Lemon, Nutty, Pepper, Ginger, Oak, Vanilla, Caramel, Tobacco, Leather, Spice, Butter, Wax, Bread, Bacon, Medicinal, Earth, Peaty

THE WHISKEY TASTING DOODLE BOOK™

TASTE - OK, now take a sip. Roll it around. Describe it.

1. FIRST TASTE

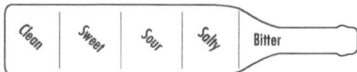

Clean | Sweet | Sour | Salty | Bitter

2. FLAVOR

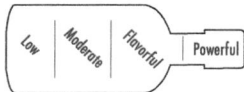

Low | Moderate | Flavorful | Powerful

3. PEATY

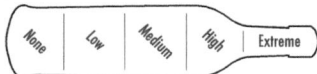

None | Low | Medium | High | Extreme

4. BODY

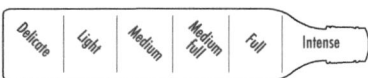

Delicate | Light | Medium | Medium full | Full | Intense

5. SWEETNESS

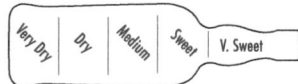

Very Dry | Dry | Medium | Sweet | V. Sweet

DOODLES & NOTES

6. FLAVOR GRAPH

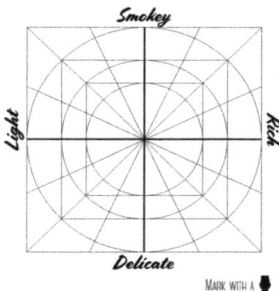

Smokey

Light

Rich

Delicate

MARK WITH A ⬥

7. FINISH

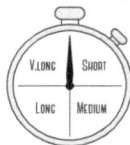

V. LONG | SHORT
LONG | MEDIUM

Describe it

8. BALANCE

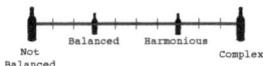

Not Balanced | Balanced | Harmonious | Complex

9. DEPTH

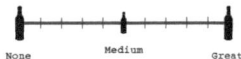

None | Medium | Great

10. OFF-FLAVORS?

OTHER THOUGHTS - What did you think of this one?

BOTTLE & LABEL

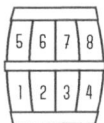

5 | 6 | 7 | 8
1 | 2 | 3 | 4

VALUE

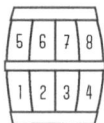

5 | 6 | 7 | 8
1 | 2 | 3 | 4

PRICE

DRINK AGAIN?

DESCRIBE IN 3 WORDS

_____

_____

_____

LOG:

Distillery _____ Region _____

Whiskey Name _____ Country _____

Type _____ ABV _____

Age _____ Unicorn? 👍 Rating 🥃 🥃 🥃 🥃 🥃

APPEARANCE – First, fill your glass! (Or draw your own)

| Swirling Glass | Vinum Single Malt | Large Glencairn | NEAT Glass | Wine | Glencairn | Straight Tumbler | Bourbon Tumbler | Draw Your Own! |

Now, hold it up against a white background. Describe what you see.

1. CLARITY

Watery, Pale — Medium — Opaque, Deep

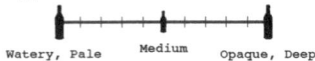

2. VISCOSITY / LEGS

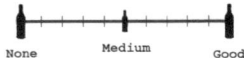

None — Medium — Good

3. COLOR & HUE

Lighter
ld/Amber
Darker

Gin Clear	Pale Straw	Light Gold
Yellow Gold	Golden	Pale Amber
Rich Amber	Burnt Amber	Tawny
Mahogany	Old Oak	Treacle

4. DOODLES & NOTES

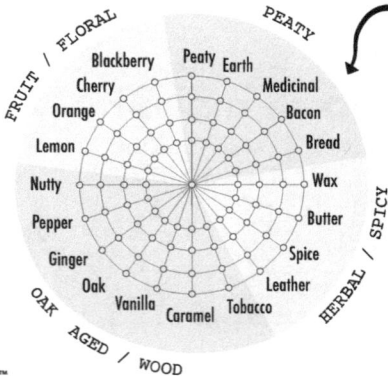

AROMA – Let's get your nose involved. Use the Aroma Wheel.

DOODLES & NOTES

Aroma Wheel:

FRUIT / FLORAL — PEATY — HERBAL / SPICY — OAK AGED / WOOD

Blackberry, Cherry, Orange, Lemon, Nutty, Pepper, Ginger, Oak, Vanilla, Caramel, Tobacco, Leather, Spice, Butter, Wax, Bread, Bacon, Medicinal, Earth, Peaty

THE WHISKEY TASTING DOODLE BOOK™

TASTE - OK, now take a sip. Roll it around. Describe it.

1. FIRST TASTE

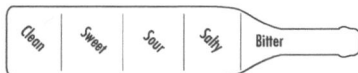

Clean | Sweet | Sour | Salty | Bitter

2. FLAVOR

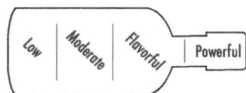

Low | Moderate | Flavorful | Powerful

3. PEATY

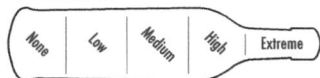

None | Low | Medium | High | Extreme

4. BODY

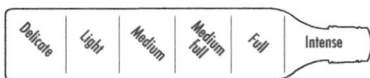

Delicate | Light | Medium | Medium full | Full | Intense

5. SWEETNESS

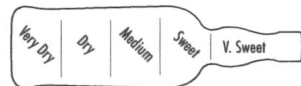

Very Dry | Dry | Medium | Sweet | V. Sweet

DOODLES & NOTES

6. FLAVOR GRAPH

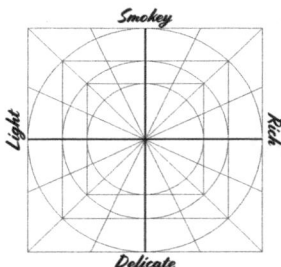

Smokey

Light

Rich

Delicate

MARK WITH A 🍾

7. FINISH

V. LONG | SHORT
LONG | MEDIUM

Describe it

8. BALANCE

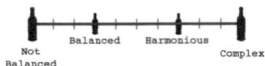

Not Balanced | Balanced | Harmonious | Complex

9. DEPTH

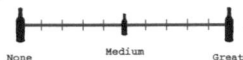

None | Medium | Great

10. OFF-FLAVORS?

OTHER THOUGHTS - What did you think of this one?

BOTTLE & LABEL

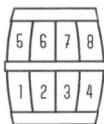

5 6 7 8
1 2 3 4

VALUE

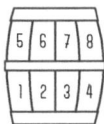

5 6 7 8
1 2 3 4

PRICE

DRINK AGAIN?

DESCRIBE IN 3 WORDS

_____
_____
_____

THE WHISKEY TASTING DOODLE BOOK™

LOG:

Distillery _____ Region _____

Whiskey Name _____ Country _____

Type _____ ABV _____

Age _____ Unicorn? 👍 Rating 🥃🥃🥃🥃🥃

APPEARANCE -First, fill your glass! (Or draw your own)

| Swirling Glass | Vinum Single Malt | Large Glencairn | NEAT Glass | Wine | Glencairn | Straight Tumbler | Bourbon Tumbler | Draw Your Own! |

Now, hold it up against a white background. Describe what you see.

1. CLARITY

Watery, Pale — Medium — Opaque, Deep

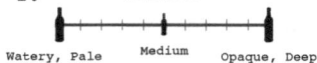

2. VISCOSITY / LEGS

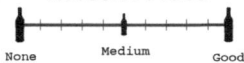

None — Medium — Good

3. COLOR & HUE

Lighter / d/Amber / Darker

Gin Clear	Pale Straw	Light Gold
Yellow Gold	Golden	Pale Amber
Rich Amber	Burnt Amber	Tawny
Mahogany	Old Oak	Treacle

4. DOODLES & NOTES

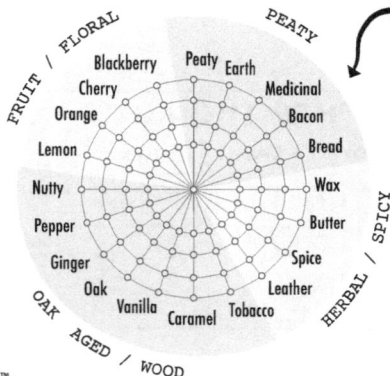

AROMA - Let's get your nose involved. Use the Aroma Wheel.

DOODLES & NOTES

FRUIT / FLORAL — PEATY — HERBAL / SPICY — OAK / AGED / WOOD

Blackberry, Cherry, Orange, Lemon, Nutty, Pepper, Ginger, Oak, Vanilla, Caramel, Tobacco, Leather, Spice, Butter, Wax, Bread, Bacon, Medicinal, Earth, Peaty

THE WHISKEY TASTING DOODLE BOOK™

TASTE - OK, now take a sip. Roll it around. Describe it.

1. FIRST TASTE

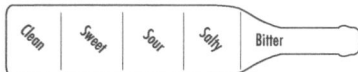

Clean | Sweet | Sour | Salty | Bitter

2. FLAVOR

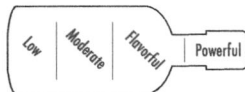

Low | Moderate | Flavorful | Powerful

3. PEATY

None | Low | Medium | High | Extreme

4. BODY

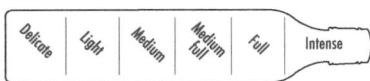

Delicate | Light | Medium | Medium Full | Full | Intense

5. SWEETNESS

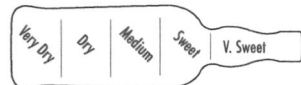

Very Dry | Dry | Medium | Sweet | V. Sweet

DOODLES & NOTES

6. FLAVOR GRAPH

Smokey | Light | Rich | Delicate

MARK WITH A ●

7. FINISH

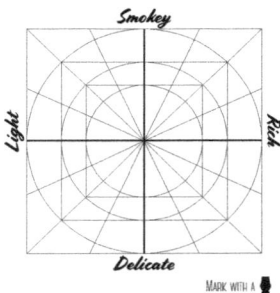

V.Long | Short | Long | Medium

Describe it

8. BALANCE

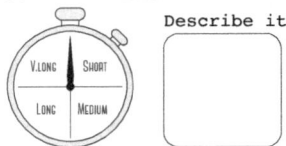

Not Balanced | Balanced | Harmonious | Complex

9. DEPTH

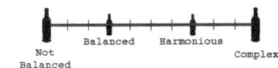

None | Medium | Great

10. OFF-FLAVORS?

OTHER THOUGHTS - What did you think of this one?

BOTTLE & LABEL

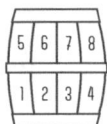

5 6 7 8
1 2 3 4

VALUE

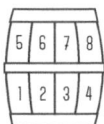

5 6 7 8
1 2 3 4

PRICE

DRINK AGAIN?

DESCRIBE IN 3 WORDS

_____
_____
_____

THE WHISKEY TASTING DOODLE BOOK™

LOG:

Distillery _____ Region _____

Whiskey Name _____ Country _____

Type _____ ABV _____

Age _____ Unicorn? 👍 Rating 🥃 🥃 🥃 🥃 🥃

APPEARANCE - First, fill your glass! (Or draw your own)

Swirling Glass | Visun Single Malt | Large Glencairn | NEAT Glass | Wine | Glencairn | Straight Tumbler | Bourbon Tumbler | Draw Your Own!

Now, hold it up against a white background. Describe what you see

1.   CLARITY

Watery, Pale | Medium | Opaque, Deep

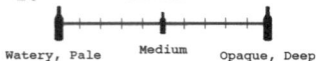

2.   VISCOSITY / LEGS

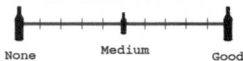

None | Medium | Good

3.   COLOR & HUE

Lighter / Gold/Amber / Darker

Gin Clear	Pale Straw	Light Gold
Yellow Gold	Golden	Pale Amber
Rich Amber	Burnt Amber	Tawny
Mahogany	Old Oak	Treacle

4.   DOODLES & NOTES

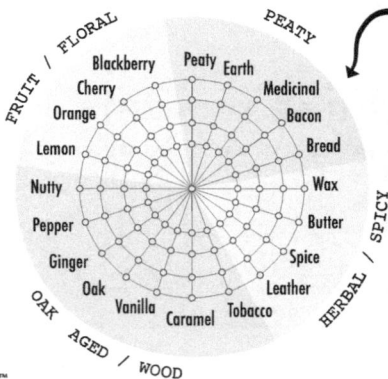

AROMA - Let's get your nose involved. Use the Aroma Wheel.

DOODLES & NOTES

FRUIT / FLORAL — PEATY — HERBAL / SPICY — OAK AGED / WOOD

Blackberry, Cherry, Orange, Lemon, Nutty, Pepper, Ginger, Oak, Vanilla, Caramel, Tobacco, Leather, Spice, Butter, Wax, Bread, Bacon, Medicinal, Earth, Peaty

THE WHISKEY TASTING DOODLE BOOK™

TASTE - OK, now take a sip. Roll it around. Describe it.

1. FIRST TASTE

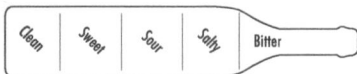

Clean | Sweet | Sour | Salty | Bitter

2. FLAVOR

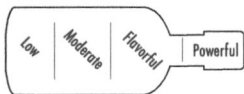

Low | Moderate | Flavorful | Powerful

3. PEATY

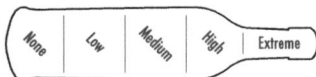

None | Low | Medium | High | Extreme

4. BODY

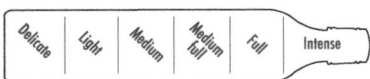

Delicate | Light | Medium | Medium full | Full | Intense

5. SWEETNESS

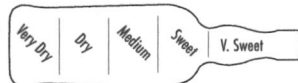

Very Dry | Dry | Medium | Sweet | V. Sweet

DOODLES & NOTES

6. FLAVOR GRAPH

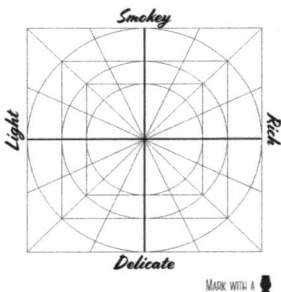

Smokey

Light

Rich

Delicate

MARK WITH A ●

7. FINISH

V.LONG | SHORT
LONG | MEDIUM

Describe it

8. BALANCE

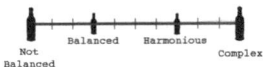

Not Balanced | Balanced | Harmonious | Complex

9. DEPTH

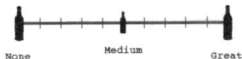

None | Medium | Great

10. OFF-FLAVORS?

OTHER THOUGHTS - What did you think of this one?

BOTTLE & LABEL

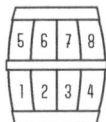

5 | 6 | 7 | 8
1 | 2 | 3 | 4

VALUE

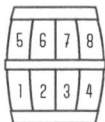

5 | 6 | 7 | 8
1 | 2 | 3 | 4

PRICE

DRINK AGAIN?

DESCRIBE IN 3 WORDS

LOG:

Distillery _____   Region _____

Whiskey Name _____   Country _____

Type _____   ABV _____

Age _____   Unicorn? 👍   Rating 🥃🥃🥃🥃🥃

APPEARANCE – First, fill your glass! (Or draw your own)

Swirling Glass | Vinum Single Malt | Large Glencairn | NEAT Glass | Wine | Glencairn | Straight Tumbler | Bourbon Tumbler | Draw Your Own!

Now, hold it up against a white background. Describe what you see

1. CLARITY

Watery, Pale — Medium — Opaque, Deep

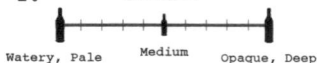

2. VISCOSITY / LEGS

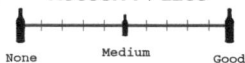

None — Medium — Good

3. COLOR & HUE

Lighter / Gold/Amber / Darker

Gin Clear	Pale Straw	Light Gold
Yellow Gold	Golden	Pale Amber
Rich Amber	Burnt Amber	Tawny
Mahogany	Old Oak	Treacle

4. DOODLES & NOTES

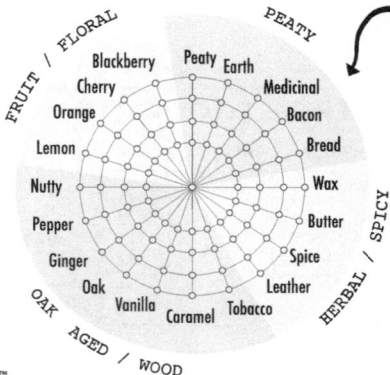

AROMA – Let's get your nose involved. Use the Aroma Wheel.

DOODLES & NOTES

FRUIT / FLORAL

PEATY

Blackberry
Cherry
Orange
Lemon
Nutty
Pepper
Ginger
Oak
Vanilla
Caramel

Peaty Earth
Medicinal
Bacon
Bread
Wax
Butter
Spice
Leather
Tobacco

HERBAL / SPICY

OAK AGED / WOOD

THE WHISKEY TASTING DOODLE BOOK™

TASTE - OK, now take a sip. Roll it around. Describe it.

1. FIRST TASTE

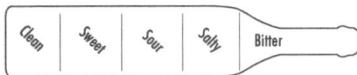

Clean | Sweet | Sour | Salty | Bitter

2. FLAVOR

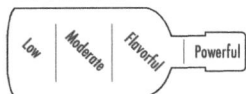

Low | Moderate | Flavorful | Powerful

3. PEATY

None | Low | Medium | High | Extreme

4. BODY

Delicate | Light | Medium | Medium full | Full | Intense

5. SWEETNESS

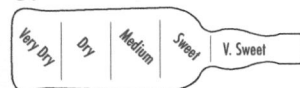

Very Dry | Dry | Medium | Sweet | V. Sweet

DOODLES & NOTES

6. FLAVOR GRAPH

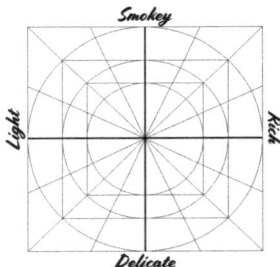

Smokey · Light · Rich · Delicate

MARK WITH A 🔴

7. FINISH

V. Long | Short | Long | Medium

Describe it

8. BALANCE

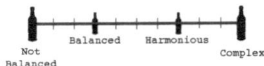

Not Balanced | Balanced | Harmonious | Complex

9. DEPTH

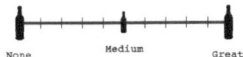

None | Medium | Great

10. OFF-FLAVORS?

OTHER THOUGHTS - What did you think of this one?

BOTTLE & LABEL

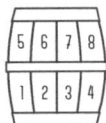

5 | 6 | 7 | 8
1 | 2 | 3 | 4

VALUE

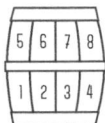

5 | 6 | 7 | 8
1 | 2 | 3 | 4

PRICE

DRINK AGAIN?

DESCRIBE IN 3 WORDS

_____
_____
_____

LOG:

Distillery _____   Region _____

Whiskey Name _____   Country _____

Type _____   ABV _____

Age _____   Unicorn? 👍   Rating ♢ ♢ ♢ ♢ ♢

APPEARANCE – First, fill your glass! (Or draw your own)

Swirling Glass | Vinum Single Malt | Large Glencairn | NEAT Glass | Wine | Glencairn | Straight Tumbler | Bourbon Tumbler | Draw Your Own!

Now, hold it up against a white background. Describe what you see

1.   CLARITY

Watery, Pale — Medium — Opaque, Deep

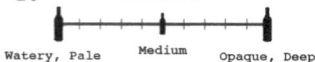

2.   VISCOSITY / LEGS

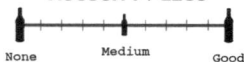

None — Medium — Good

3.   COLOR & HUE

Lighter
Gold/Amber
Darker

Gin Clear	Pale Straw	Light Gold
Yellow Gold	Golden	Pale Amber
Rich Amber	Burnt Amber	Tawny
Mahogany	Old Oak	Treacle

4.   DOODLES & NOTES

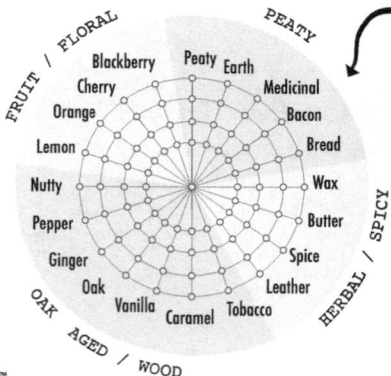

AROMA – Let's get your nose involved. Use the Aroma Wheel.

DOODLES & NOTES

FRUIT / FLORAL — PEATY — HERBAL / SPICY — OAK AGED / WOOD

Blackberry, Cherry, Orange, Lemon, Nutty, Pepper, Ginger, Oak, Vanilla, Caramel, Tobacco, Leather, Spice, Butter, Wax, Bread, Bacon, Medicinal, Earth, Peaty

TASTE - OK, now take a sip. Roll it around. Describe it.

1. FIRST TASTE
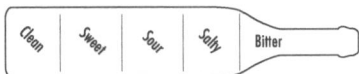
Clean | Sweet | Sour | Salty | Bitter

2. FLAVOR
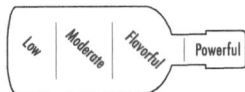
Low | Moderate | Flavorful | Powerful

3. PEATY
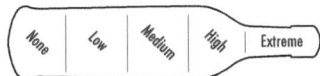
None | Low | Medium | High | Extreme

4. BODY
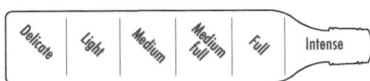
Delicate | Light | Medium | Medium full | Full | Intense

5. SWEETNESS
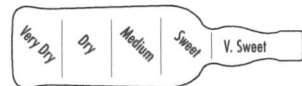
Very Dry | Dry | Medium | Sweet | V. Sweet

DOODLES & NOTES

6. FLAVOR GRAPH
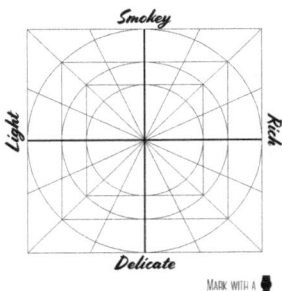
Smokey — Light — Rich — Delicate
MARK WITH A

7. FINISH
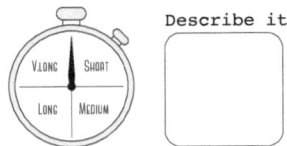
V.Long | Short | Long | Medium
Describe it

8. BALANCE
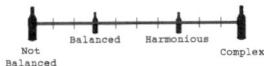
Not Balanced | Balanced | Harmonious | Complex

9. DEPTH
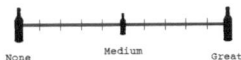
None | Medium | Great

10. OFF-FLAVORS?

OTHER THOUGHTS - What did you think of this one?

BOTTLE & LABEL
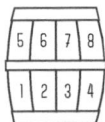
5 | 6 | 7 | 8
1 | 2 | 3 | 4

VALUE
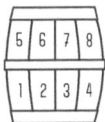
5 | 6 | 7 | 8
1 | 2 | 3 | 4

PRICE

DRINK AGAIN?

DESCRIBE IN 3 WORDS

LOG:

Distillery _____ Region _____

Whiskey Name _____ Country _____

Type _____ ABV _____

Age _____ Unicorn? 👍 Rating 🥃🥃🥃🥃🥃

APPEARANCE - First, fill your glass! (Or draw your own)

Swirling Glass | Vinum Single Malt | Large Glencairn | NEAT Glass | Wine | Glencairn | Straight Tumbler | Bourbon Tumbler | Draw Your Own!

Now, hold it up against a white background. Describe what you see.

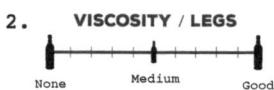

1. CLARITY

Watery, Pale — Medium — Opaque, Deep

2. VISCOSITY / LEGS

None — Medium — Good

3. COLOR & HUE

Lighter
ld/Amber
Darker

Gin Clear	Pale Straw	Light Gold
Yellow Gold	Golden	Pale Amber
Rich Amber	Burnt Amber	Tawny
Mahogany	Old Oak	Treacle

4. DOODLES & NOTES

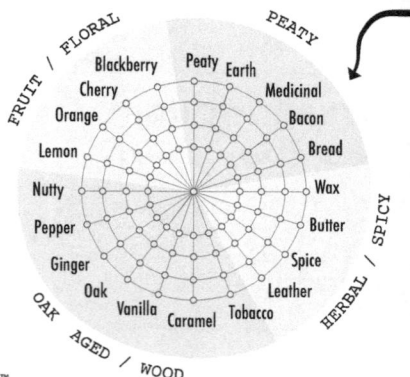

AROMA - Let's get your nose involved. Use the Aroma Wheel.

DOODLES & NOTES

FRUIT / FLORAL — PEATY — HERBAL / SPICY — OAK AGED / WOOD

Blackberry, Cherry, Orange, Lemon, Nutty, Pepper, Ginger, Oak, Vanilla, Caramel, Tobacco, Leather, Spice, Butter, Wax, Bread, Bacon, Medicinal, Earth, Peaty

THE WHISKEY TASTING DOODLE BOOK™

TASTE - OK, now take a sip. Roll it around. Describe it.

1. FIRST TASTE

Clean | Sweet | Sour | Salty | Bitter

2. FLAVOR

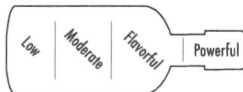

Low | Moderate | Flavorful | Powerful

3. PEATY

None | Low | Medium | High | Extreme

4. BODY

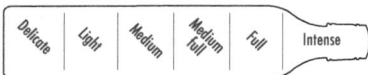

Delicate | Light | Medium | Medium full | Full | Intense

5. SWEETNESS

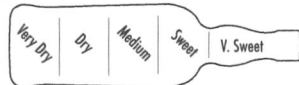

Very Dry | Dry | Medium | Sweet | V. Sweet

DOODLES & NOTES

6. FLAVOR GRAPH

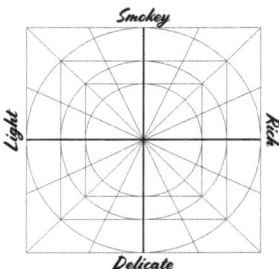

Smokey

Light

Rich

Delicate

MARK WITH A 🖤

7. FINISH

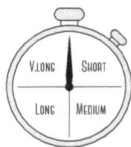

V.LONG | SHORT
LONG | MEDIUM

Describe it

8. BALANCE

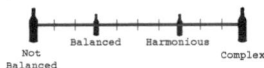

Not Balanced | Balanced | Harmonious | Complex

9. DEPTH

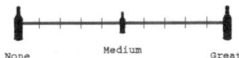

None | Medium | Great

10. OFF-FLAVORS?

OTHER THOUGHTS - What did you think of this one?

BOTTLE & LABEL

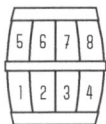

5 | 6 | 7 | 8
1 | 2 | 3 | 4

VALUE

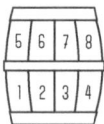

5 | 6 | 7 | 8
1 | 2 | 3 | 4

PRICE

DRINK AGAIN?

DESCRIBE IN 3 WORDS

_____
_____
_____

LOG:

Distillery _____   Region _____

Whiskey Name _____   Country _____

Type _____   ABV _____

Age _____   Unicorn? 👍   Rating 🥃🥃🥃🥃🥃

APPEARANCE - First, fill your glass! (Or draw your own)

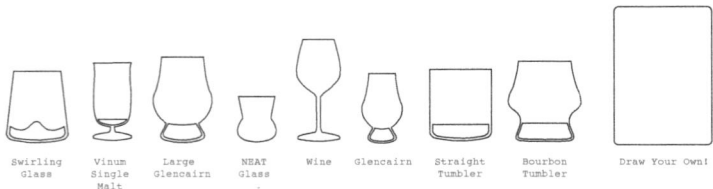

Swirling Glass | Vinum Single Malt | Large Glencairn | NEAT Glass | Wine | Glencairn | Straight Tumbler | Bourbon Tumbler | Draw Your Own!

Now, hold it up against a white background. Describe what you see.

1.   CLARITY

Watery, Pale — Medium — Opaque, Deep

2.   VISCOSITY / LEGS

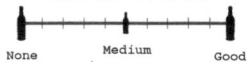

None — Medium — Good

3.   COLOR & HUE

Lighter
Gold/Amber
Darker

Gin Clear	Pale Straw	Light Gold
Yellow Gold	Golden	Pale Amber
Rich Amber	Burnt Amber	Tawny
Mahogany	Old Oak	Treacle

4.   DOODLES & NOTES

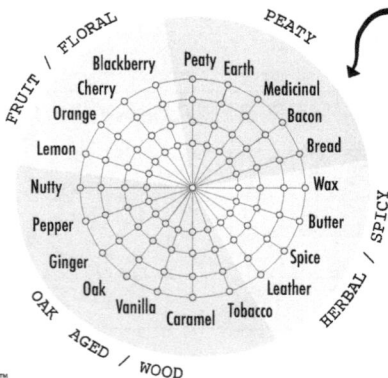

AROMA - Let's get your nose involved. Use the Aroma Wheel.

DOODLES & NOTES

FRUIT / FLORAL   PEATY

Blackberry   Peaty   Earth
Cherry   Medicinal
Orange   Bacon
Lemon   Bread
Nutty   Wax
Pepper   Butter
Ginger   Spice
Oak   Leather
Vanilla   Caramel   Tobacco

OAK AGED / WOOD   HERBAL / SPICY

THE WHISKEY TASTING DOODLE BOOK™

TASTE - OK, now take a sip. Roll it around. Describe it.

1. FIRST TASTE

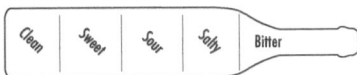

Clean | Sweet | Sour | Salty | Bitter

2. FLAVOR

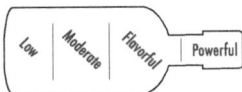

Low | Moderate | Flavorful | Powerful

3. PEATY

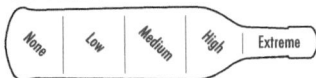

None | Low | Medium | High | Extreme

4. BODY

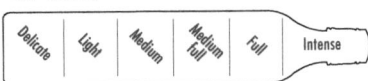

Delicate | Light | Medium | Medium full | Full | Intense

5. SWEETNESS

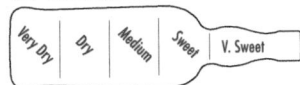

Very Dry | Dry | Medium | Sweet | V. Sweet

DOODLES & NOTES

6. FLAVOR GRAPH

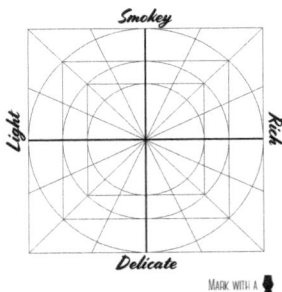

Smokey

Light

Rich

Delicate

MARK WITH A ●

7. FINISH

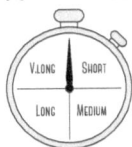

V. LONG | SHORT | LONG | MEDIUM

Describe it

8. BALANCE

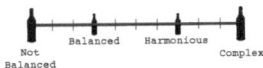

Not Balanced | Balanced | Harmonious | Complex

9. DEPTH

None | Medium | Great

10. OFF-FLAVORS?

OTHER THOUGHTS - What did you think of this one?

BOTTLE & LABEL

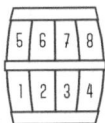

5 | 6 | 7 | 8
1 | 2 | 3 | 4

VALUE

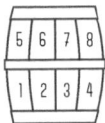

5 | 6 | 7 | 8
1 | 2 | 3 | 4

PRICE

DRINK AGAIN?

DESCRIBE IN 3 WORDS

_____

_____

_____

LOG:

Distillery _____	Region _____
Whiskey Name _____	Country _____
Type _____	ABV _____
Age _____ Unicorn? 👍	Rating 🥃🥃🥃🥃🥃

APPEARANCE — First, fill your glass! (Or draw your own)

| Swirling Glass | Vinum Single Malt | Large Glencairn | NEAT Glass | Wine | Glencairn | Straight Tumbler | Bourbon Tumbler | Draw Your Own! |

Now, hold it up against a white background. Describe what you see

1.   CLARITY

Watery, Pale   Medium   Opaque, Deep

2.   VISCOSITY / LEGS

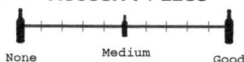

None   Medium   Good

3.   COLOR & HUE

Lighter
Gold/Amber
Darker

Gin Clear	Pale Straw	Light Gold
Yellow Gold	Golden	Pale Amber
Rich Amber	Burnt Amber	Tawny
Mahogany	Old Oak	Treacle

4.   DOODLES & NOTES

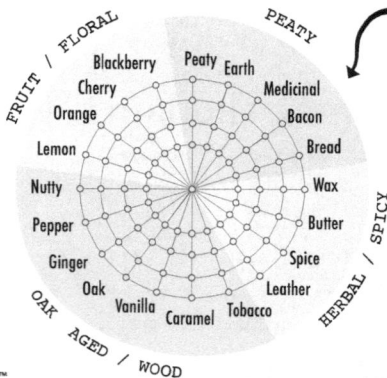

AROMA — Let's get your nose involved. Use the Aroma Wheel.

DOODLES & NOTES

Aroma Wheel labels:
FRUIT / FLORAL — Blackberry, Cherry, Orange, Lemon, Nutty, Pepper, Ginger
PEATY — Peaty, Earth, Medicinal, Bacon, Bread, Wax, Butter
HERBAL / SPICY — Spice, Leather, Tobacco
OAK AGED / WOOD — Oak, Vanilla, Caramel

THE WHISKEY TASTING DOODLE BOOK™

TASTE - OK, now take a sip. Roll it around. Describe it.

1. FIRST TASTE

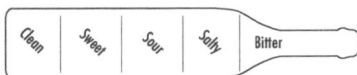

Clean | Sweet | Sour | Salty | Bitter

2. FLAVOR

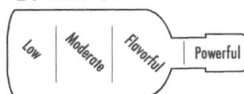

Low | Moderate | Flavorful | Powerful

3. PEATY

None | Low | Medium | High | Extreme

4. BODY

Delicate | Light | Medium | Medium Full | Full | Intense

5. SWEETNESS

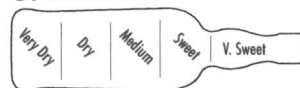

Very Dry | Dry | Medium | Sweet | V. Sweet

DOODLES & NOTES

6. FLAVOR GRAPH

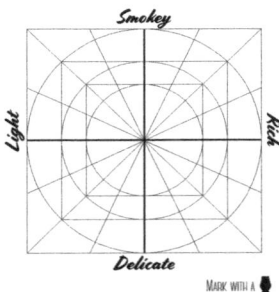

Smokey

Light

Rich

Delicate

MARK WITH A ●

7. FINISH

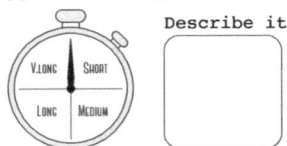

V. LONG | SHORT
LONG | MEDIUM

Describe it

8. BALANCE

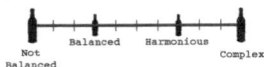

Not Balanced | Balanced | Harmonious | Complex

9. DEPTH

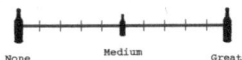

None | Medium | Great

10. OFF-FLAVORS?

OTHER THOUGHTS - What did you think of this one?

BOTTLE & LABEL

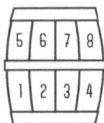

5 | 6 | 7 | 8
1 | 2 | 3 | 4

VALUE

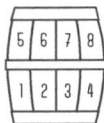

5 | 6 | 7 | 8
1 | 2 | 3 | 4

PRICE

DRINK AGAIN?

DESCRIBE IN 3 WORDS

_____

_____

_____

THE WHISKEY TASTING DOODLE BOOK™

LOG:

Distillery _____	Region _____
Whiskey Name _____	Country _____
Type _____	ABV _____
Age _____	Unicorn? 👍	Rating 🥃🥃🥃🥃🥃

APPEARANCE - First, fill your glass! (Or draw your own)

| Swirling Glass | Vinum Single Malt | Large Glencairn | NEAT Glass | Wine | Glencairn | Straight Tumbler | Bourbon Tumbler | Draw Your Own! |

Now, hold it up against a white background. Describe what you see.

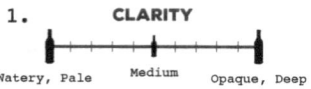

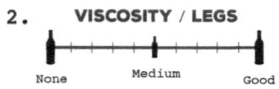

1. CLARITY

Watery, Pale   Medium   Opaque, Deep

2. VISCOSITY / LEGS

None   Medium   Good

3. COLOR & HUE

Lighter / d/Amber / Darker

Gin Clear	Pale Straw	Light Gold
Yellow Gold	Golden	Pale Amber
Rich Amber	Burnt Amber	Tawny
Mahogany	Old Oak	Treacle

4. DOODLES & NOTES

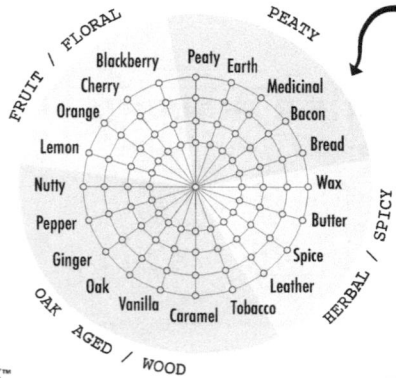

AROMA - Let's get your nose involved. Use the Aroma Wheel.

DOODLES & NOTES

FRUIT / FLORAL — PEATY

Blackberry, Peaty, Earth
Cherry, Medicinal
Orange, Bacon
Lemon, Bread
Nutty, Wax
Pepper, Butter
Ginger, Spice
Oak, Leather
Vanilla, Caramel, Tobacco

HERBAL / SPICY

OAK AGED / WOOD

TASTE - OK, now take a sip. Roll it around. Describe it.

1. FIRST TASTE

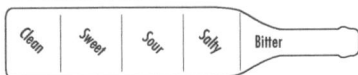
Clean | Sweet | Sour | Salty | Bitter

2. FLAVOR

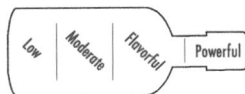
Low | Moderate | Flavorful | Powerful

3. PEATY

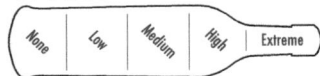
None | Low | Medium | High | Extreme

4. BODY

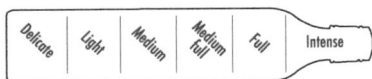
Delicate | Light | Medium | Medium full | Full | Intense

5. SWEETNESS

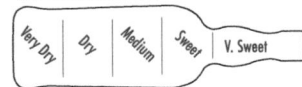
Very Dry | Dry | Medium | Sweet | V. Sweet

DOODLES & NOTES

6. FLAVOR GRAPH

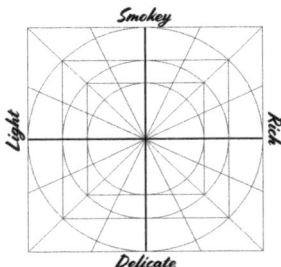
Smokey
Light
Rich
Delicate
MARK WITH A ●

7. FINISH

V.LONG | SHORT
LONG | MEDIUM

Describe it

8. BALANCE

Not Balanced | Balanced | Harmonious | Complex

9. DEPTH

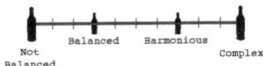
None | Medium | Great

10. OFF-FLAVORS?

OTHER THOUGHTS - What did you think of this one?

BOTTLE & LABEL

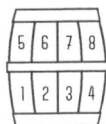
5 | 6 | 7 | 8
1 | 2 | 3 | 4

VALUE

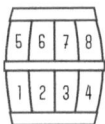
5 | 6 | 7 | 8
1 | 2 | 3 | 4

PRICE

DRINK AGAIN?

DESCRIBE IN 3 WORDS

_____

_____

_____

LOG:

1.

2.

3.

4.

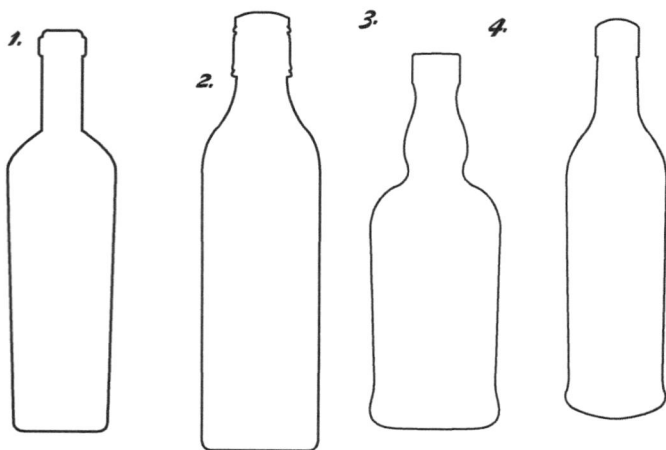

DOODLE YOUR FAVORITE WHISKEY BOTTLES

Or create your own

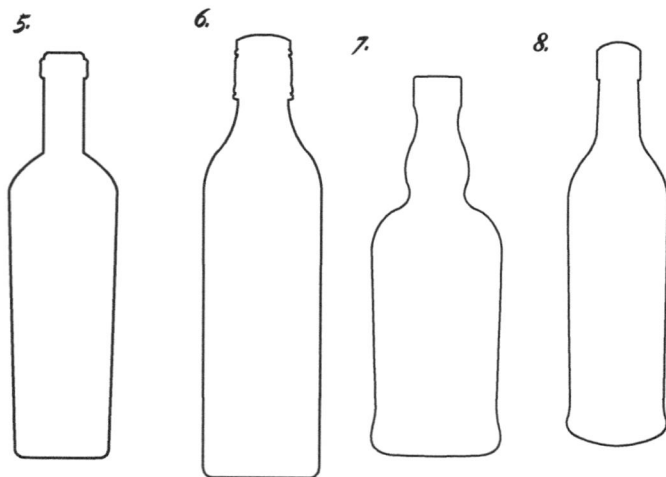

5.

6.

7.

8.

BOTTLE DOODLE PAGE

Express Your Ideas

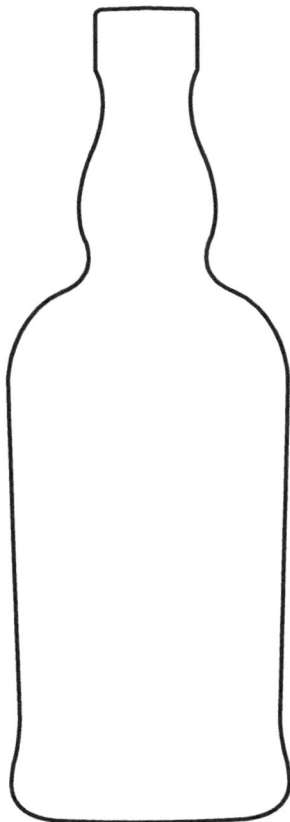

DOODLES & NOTES

BOTTLE DOODLE PAGE

Artistic Notes

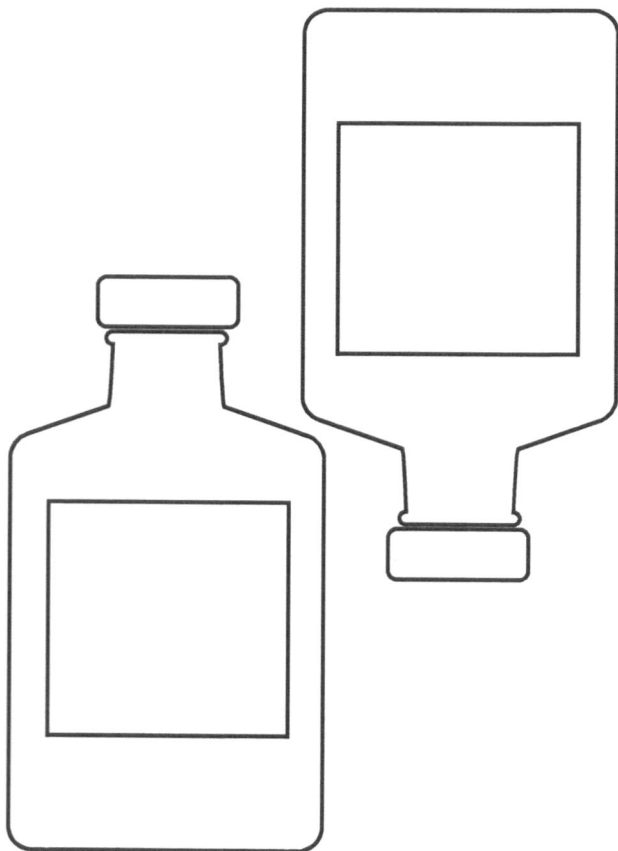

DOODLES & NOTES

BOTTLE DOODLE PAGE

Tap Your Creativity

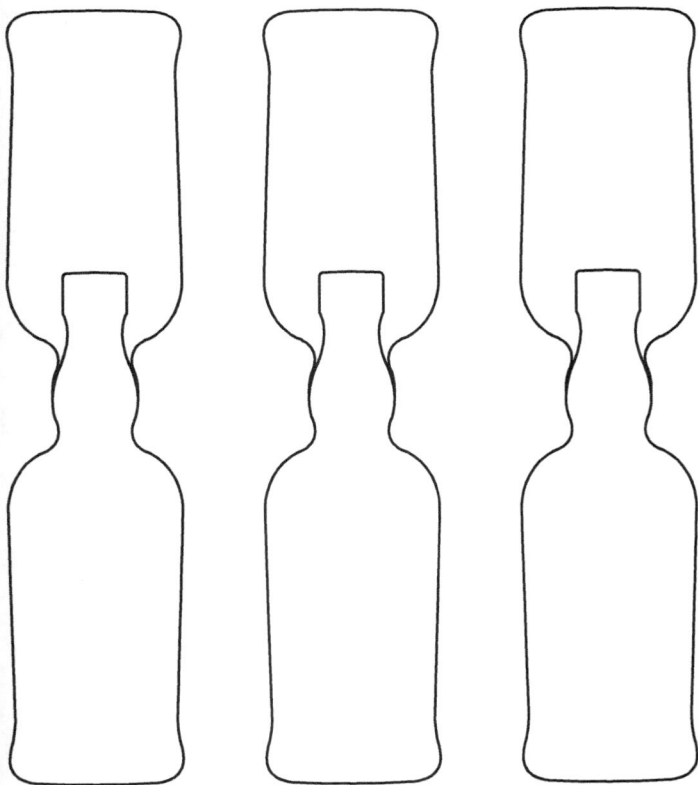

DOODLES & NOTES

BOTTLE DOODLE PAGE

Doodle what you like

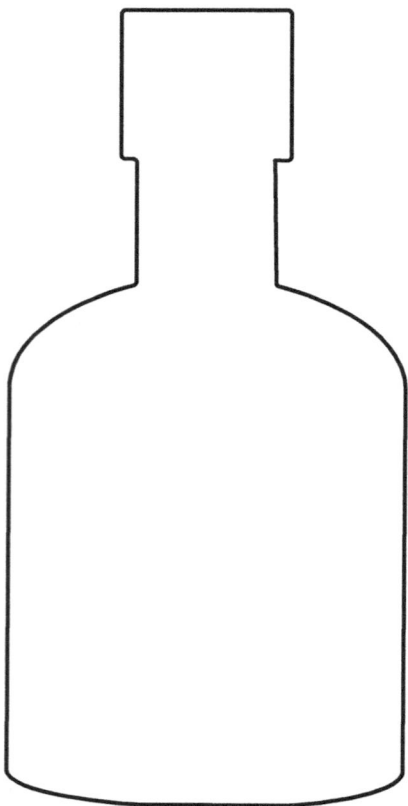

DOODLES & NOTES

CHECK OUT OUR OTHER DOODLE BOOKS
AND MORE AWESOME PRODUCTS AT

WWW.ARTISANDOODLEBOOKS.COM

WE ARE A

HOME
BREW
DEPOT
LOS ANGELES

COMPANY

THANK YOU FOR YOUR SUPPORT!
FOLLOW US @HOMEBREWDEPOTLA